Kundalini Energy

Beginner's Guide to Open Your Third Eye Chakra, Increase Awareness, Enhance Psychic Abilities and Awaken Your Energetic Potential

Elizabeth Wood

© Copyright 2020 by Elizabeth Wood. All rights reserved.

The work contained herein has been produced with the intent to provide relevant knowledge and information on the topic described in the title for entertainment purposes only. While the author has gone to every extent to furnish up to date and true information, no claims can be made as to its accuracy or validity as the author has made no claims to be an expert on this topic. Notwithstanding, the reader is asked to do their own research and consult any subject matter experts they deem necessary to ensure the quality and accuracy of the material presented herein.

This statement is legally binding as deemed by the Committee of Publishers Association and the American Bar Association for the territory of the United States. Other jurisdictions may apply their own legal statutes. Any reproduction, transmission or copying of this material contained in this work without the express written consent of the copyright holder shall be deemed as a copyright violation as per the current legislation in force on the date of publishing and subsequent time thereafter. All additional works derived from this material may be claimed by the holder of this copyright.

The data, depictions, events, descriptions and all other information forthwith are considered to be true, fair and accurate unless the work is expressly described as a work of fiction. Regardless of the nature of this work, the Publisher is exempt from any responsibility of actions taken by the reader in conjunction with this work. The Publisher acknowledges that the reader acts of their own accord and releases the author and Publisher of any responsibility for the observance of tips, advice, counsel, strategies and techniques that may be offered in this volume.

TABLE OF CONTENTS

INTRODUCTION 1

CHAPTER 1 *Kundalini Energy* 2

   What Is Kundalini Energy 2

   Where Does Kundalini Come From 4

   History of the Kundalini 5

CHAPTER 2 *The Purpose Of Kundalini Energy* 7

   Integrate Your Soul 7

   Release Your Potential 9

   Awaken Your Divine Purpose 11

CHAPTER 3 *The Benefits Of Kundalini EnergY* 13

   Personal Peace 13

   Enhanced Psychic Ability 15

   Increased Creativity 17

   Better Spiritual Connections 19

   Additional Benefits to Awakening Your Kundalini 20

CHAPTER 4 *Obstacles To Achieving Kundalini Energy* 23

CHAPTER 5 *The Ten Bodies Of Kundalini Yoga* 27

CHAPTER 6 *Symptoms Of Kundalini Awakening* 31

   Rush of Energy 31

   A Desire for Peace and Calm 32

Changes in Sleep Habits 33

Stronger Connection With Nature 33

Positivity Through a Positive Mind 34

CHAPTER 7 *Awakening Kundalini Through Your Chakras* 36

The Seven Chakras 37

CHAPTER 8 *How To Awaken The Kundalini* 43

Meditation and Breathing 43

Crystal Therapy 48

Kundalini Yoga 51

Oils and Aromas 53

CHAPTER 9 *Life With Kundalini Energy* 56

Intuition 56

Psychic Ability 58

Divinity and the Divine 61

Knowledge of Angels and Spirits 62

Seeing the Aura of Others 64

Visiting Parallel Dimensions 67

Life After Life 69

Communicating With Others 71

CONCLUSION 73

DESCRIPTION 75

INTRODUCTION

Congratulations on purchasing *Kundalini Energy,* and thank you for doing so.

The following chapters will discuss the energy of the Kundalini and how you can put this energy to work in your life. This energy is something that has been with you since birth, lying quietly asleep, waiting for the day when you decided you needed its power to improve your life. Maybe you've heard about the energy of the Kundalini, and you want to harness it for your use. Perhaps this is the first time you've heard about it, and you are curious. Whatever the reason you want to know about Kundalini energy, now is the time to learn.

Kundalini energy is the force of the divine working within you. It is the secret power that will take your life to the ultimate level of transformation. When you awaken your Kundalini and release the energy waiting within, you will be the recipient of a level of self-realization that will put you in touch with the Divine and all the mysteries of the universe and other worlds. It is your connection with the other inhabitants of the universe. It is the key to fully realizing your true potential. It comes from the Divine, and it will connect you to the Divine.

Ancient literature described this energy for thousands of years. Different names in different teachings represent it, but it is all the same sustaining force. This journey you are about to begin will take you to places you have never been to before. You will now have the power that you have never known before. You will become the most decisive person spiritually and emotionally that you have ever been.

There are plenty of books on this subject on the market; thanks again for choosing this one! Every effort was made to ensure it is full of as much useful information as possible; please enjoy!

CHAPTER 1
Kundalini Energy

Kundalini energy is the source of all power in the universe. Inside every person is a subtle life system that nurtures you and protects your body, mind, and soul. This energy is with you when you are born, and it will be with you when you die. It lies dormant until you decide to awaken it. Then it flows through your body and elevates you to levels never before known to you. This ancient energy is unbeatable, as well as being perfect and pure. Like a fire inside you, it burns away the impurities and cleanses your imperfections with its all-consuming power.

What Is Kundalini Energy

Kundalini is a term that originated in ancient India from Sanskrit. The name identifies the rising of consciousness and energy that has been lying coiled at the bottom of your spine since before you were born. It is said that This is the energy of life that created the child in the womb, then it coils around the base of the child's spine three and one-half times to hold power for future use. The energy will die with that person, whether it is ever awoken and used or not. After the human's death, the energy will uncoil and return to its source in the astral plane.

Many people will live their entire lives and never make use of the powerful energy waiting inside of them. Sometimes life gets in the way. As people grow older, their attention is turned away from the inner self and the distractions of a busy world. The external aspects of a mundane life command all the public attention, and there is never enough time for awareness of a higher purpose. The energy continues to lie dormant, and the circumstances of life take over. Until the day when exploration and curiosity lead people to a place where they are ready to awaken the Kundalini, it will lay dormant and unused inside.

The Kundalini energy is the force within you that will drive your consciousness to a higher plane. It will take your attention to a place where no conscious thought will exist. It is the energy that will flow through you and wipe away your ego, so you can become the person you are meant to be. It is the power of transformation and deep awareness. It will help you break free of the fears and limiting beliefs that hold you back from realizing your full potential.

The Kundalini energy is a magical science that uses channels in your body to fill all parts of your body with life and energy. It cleanses the effects of old wounds from your aura. It will release in you a radiance that will draw in light, love, and beauty. You will know how to attract abundance into your life with the energy from the Kundalini. You will see that this abundance is your right and that listening to the words that come from your heart is the best way to live your life. You will tap into the magnetic force of the universe that brings love to everyone, and you will be grateful for the new feeling of peace in your life.

Your heart and soul will flourish because the insecurities and fears that keep you stuck in spiritual poverty will be lifted. The voice of your heart is quiet, but it is the one real voice that will lead you to your highest potential in life. Your ego often drives your mind and it will do its best to quell the words from your heart. Everything will flow well in your life when your soul and your heart are aligned. Your intuition will open, and your sensitivity will awaken. You will learn how to be present and leave behind the future's fear and the pain of the past. Your mind will no longer spin wildly out of control when you learn to calm it with the help of the Divine.

You will finally see your true worth. Awakening your Kundalini will bring you to face the self-imposed limitations that are holding you back. The challenges of life will seem less overwhelming when you can meet them with a pure heart. You will feel a confidence rising from deep within you. This confidence comes from your direct connection to the light and love flowing from the universe. This love is much deeper than your limited sense of yourself. You will manifest your most profound dreams into a fantastic reality when you feel truly worthy of success and happiness.

Letting go and living without attachments is the way of the Kundalini energy. You will integrate oneness with the universe through your soul, mind, and body. This oneness will allow you to feel a strong connection to the higher realms. The energy from these realms will remind you to recognize your oneness with the Divine and trust yourself. When you can do this, you will let go of your attachments because you will have more faith in yourself. You will begin to receive and give with energy and love. The constant chatter in your mind will be stilled, replaced by peace and calm. You will no longer need to seek approval from others because you will know that your inner truth comes from your energy and the Divine. You will attract love because you are giving love to others.

Since your real strength comes from your core energy, awakening the Kundalini energy within you will strengthen the energy flow you already know. You will develop a deep well of love for others and strong empathy for the universe with your life. You will depend on yourself and the power within you to gain the things you want in your life. Before the awakening, you are separated from your own light, but you will be your own light after the awakening.

Where Does Kundalini Come From

The Kundalini energy in your body lays tightly coiled at the bottom of your spine. Traveling up your physical backbone are three channels of life, the left channel, the right channel, and the central channel. The left channel is the magnetic feminine side, and the right track is the masculine electric side. During the Kundalini awakening, the left and right channels will unite to work in harmony with the central channel. The open central channel is physically manifested in the body by the human spine. The central channel represents the presence of your soul. This energy is the presence that unites your physical body with your soul, your subtle body. The internal chakras are laid out along the spine, going from the spine's base to the top of the head.

When you awaken the Kundalini, the energy from the spine's base will begin to travel up the central channel and through the chakras lying there. The chakras are the system of energy circuits laid out along the spine, which provide energy for your body's different parts. As the Kundalini energy travels upward, it will unblock the chakras if needed to continue its journey unimpeded. Kundalini is the full life force, full of divine energy and creative power. It is your inner fire. The ancient teachings of the yogis taught the story of the rising of Kundalini energy.

The Kundalini's energy is a sleeping goddess named Lady Shakti, waiting at the base of the spine for her reunion with Lord Shiva. As the worldly bonds are broken, and the Kundalini's energy begins to rise, Lady Shakti will begin her journey up the central channel. She brings with her all the miraculous power of the universe. She will enter the central channel's royal road, occasionally resting at the secret centers located along the way. She will finally reach the Lotus of the head and embrace the Supreme Lord Shiva in his house in the crown. Their union will create the flow of exquisite energy that will flood the body and fill it with life. If Lady Shakti remains sleeping, Lord Shiva will never have the power to bring actual knowledge to the spirit and mind. The sleeping Kundalini lies gently spiraled at the opening to the central channel, waiting for her awakening.

History of the Kundalini

Even before recorded history, there was a desire by man to believe in things unknown or unexplained. The higher power, divine beings, life after death, transcendence, supernatural powers, and magic have long been topics of interest to the common man. Every culture ever recorded has shown the presence of spiritual and religious practices. The recordings of these ancient cultures also spoke of knowledge of the Kundalini in magic and alchemy traditions. The Kundalini is believed to help one attain transcendence or acquire paranormal abilities.

Kundalini was prevalent in the Tantric traditions, known as the innate intelligence of the embodied consciousness. Early writings mention Shakti entering the central channel and bringing a vital life force upward through the body. The power of the feminine spiritual energy has a strong connection to the joy of spiritual liberation. This liberation comes as a byproduct of the union of Lady Shakti and Lord Shiva. It is seen as a type of religious experience in ancient traditions, bringing cosmic energy flowing through the body.

The concept of Kundalini energy comes from the yogic philosophy of ancient India. It refers to the kind of intelligence that works the magic of spiritual maturation and yogic awakening. It is regarded as a form of deity. In the Western mindset, Kundalini is associated with the religious practice of contemplative practices that will induce an altered state of consciousness. The appearance of the life force of energy during the Kundalini awakening is sometimes referred to as a pranic awakening. The concept of Prana is thought of as the life-sustaining vitality flowing through the body. The reservoir of subtle energy at the base of the spine is the intensified energy of life.

The ancients well understood the vast potential, pure nature, and universal power of the Kundalini. Over thousands of years, this energy, the energy of creation, was found in the Chinese, Tibetans, and the Egyptians' teachings. The sacred Vedic scriptures, education of the masters gave the first known details describing this phenomenon. It was believed to have developed in the mountains of Northern Tibet and India, in the monasteries scattered there far away from civilization. The masters passed the information along to their disciples through oral tradition. All of the techniques associated with awakening the Kundalini were meticulously practiced by students who deeply desired the chance to locate their higher selves. They wanted to awaken the serpent that would manifest its powers to produce profound results in different parts of the brain and body.

In ancient times, before the beginning of organized religion, there were no real barriers between God and man. The practices that would awaken the Kundalini, the yoga poses, breathing techniques, meditation, and mantras were sacred reminders of the connection between the body and the spirit. The goal was a direct connection with the Divine and the energetic nature of the universe. In the tradition of the Kundalini, the Divine is the source from which all energy flows freely. The Divine is part of you, but you will not be able to realize the power until you have awakened your Kundalini. Awakening your Kundalini will bring you to the transformation of self-realization.

CHAPTER 2
The Purpose Of Kundalini Energy

The purpose of awakening your Kundalini is to awaken your divine sense in the universe. You will learn to integrate your soul with your mind. You will awaken your innate potential to serve others and yourself by learning ways to love others and yourself equally. The Kundalini energy will purify and cleanse the energy systems in the body, opening them as it flows through you.

Integrate Your Soul

You might spend your days feeling very alone, even when other people surround you. Perhaps you think that no one truly understands you. You might suffer from periods of depression and anger and wonder what is wrong with you. Maybe your feelings are beginning to overwhelm you, and you desperately want to know why you feel this way for no apparent reason. Perhaps you seek something in your life, but you aren't sure where to look or even what it might be.

Your soul is seeking integration. You need to awaken your Kundalini energy so you will once again feel whole. Or maybe you have never felt genuinely complete in your life. Awakening your Kundalini will restore your faith in yourself. Once you have experienced your transformation, you will need to integrate your soul back into your previous life. Integration is the embodiment of the revelations, realizations, and wisdom you received during your Kundalini awakening. You will receive new learning during your spiritual practice that will help reveal the truth to you. You will know that something has shifted inside of you, even if the revelations and realizations are so subtle that you can barely feel them. After the awakening, you need to incorporate the new knowledge in your mind with your physical body and your soul and heart. It is all about allowing the new levels of energy and ability to flow through you unimpeded. You have learned many things during your awakening, and you will need to practice your new truths and act upon them in your new life.

There will be new levels of awareness on your spiritual planes and the emotional and psychological ones you inhabit. Some people might refer to it as walking the talk. You have a new outlook on life, and now you need to learn to live that new outlook. Integration is vital because it will connect the awareness and the knowledge to your heart. You learned things about yourself during your Kundalini awakening. Maybe you knew that you have not been very nice to the people around you. When you could genuinely see yourself without the ego wrapped around you, you might have seen the unhappy life you used to live. Before the awakening, you did not treat the people in your life with compassion and love. This empathy is part of your new awareness. When you are genuinely aware of your past actions and learn from them, you have gained wisdom. When you know from your past efforts and feel bad for the way you acted, you have understanding. The learning needs to move from your head into your heart for true wisdom to occur. You will then see that you were also hurting yourself every time you injured others in your past life. This feeling is empathy when you become aware of the pain that other people feel. You don't need to talk about your revelations and realizations, but you must do something with your new knowledge. If you don't act on your unique feelings, you can't integrate your soul into your new life.

There are things in life that defy intellect and logic. These things are more extensive than mere mortals. You can call them by any name you like, such as higher power, higher self, the source, or the god. The name you give them is not as important as realizing the energy you will receive from the Divine. You will begin to see the world in new ways, through the Third Eye and not your physical eyes. You will make the shift from collecting intellect to collecting compassion in your heart. While logic is essential, it is more important after your awakening to let your heart lead you where you need to go.

During your spiritual awakening, you will open yourself to a new level of awareness and learn to open your heart to the world. This awareness will let you feel free and allow the energy to flow freely through you. The journey through your spiritual awakening is much like peeling back the layers of an onion. You will begin to heal the many layers of you as you peel them away during your Kundalini awakening. As you start the awakening process and begin to peel away all the old layers of yourself, you will begin to feel a lightness of spirit you may not have felt in a long time, or ever. This process will also unlock all of the memories you might have repressed over the years because the experience was too painful to deal with at the time. You are full of old emotions like anger, regret, misery, hurt, and pain, feelings you have labeled as bad because they made you feel bad. Now you are peeling back the layers and exposing all of those old emotions to the light, where you will need to deal with them whether you want to or not. You will never achieve true self-realization if you do not cleanse yourself of old baggage.

This period is when you will begin to feel resistance. Even though you know you need to deal with these old emotions, you don't want to acknowledge them. You will start to feel strange feelings like confusion and fear. You once knew precisely where you were going and what you would do when you arrived, but now you aren't so sure anymore. Now you are dealing with feelings you've kept buried all these years, and they are turning your life upside down. You will doubt your lifestyle, your intelligence, and possibly even your sanity. But continuing along the path of getting rid of your ego and accepting the cleansing process of the Kundalini awakening will set you free. It is all part of the way to transformation.

When you have completed the awakening process, you will begin the soul integration. After you have awakened your spirit, you will need to bring the experience down into your physical body to ground yourself in reality again. It is not enough to do the process; you will also need to know why you are doing the procedure. Part of the process will be life changes, and these may not always be significant changes like many people expect. The small, subtle changes that happen over time usually leave the biggest lasting impression on your soul. As you become more grounded in your new life, you will become more responsive to your new feelings and awareness by accepting your new compassion and empathy. You will use your new compassion and kindness to serve humanity in many small ways. Your soul will radiate with new energy, and it will fill your life with peace. Your soul will know the plan the Divine has for it to fulfill, and it will know your place in the universe.

Release Your Potential

Awakening your Kundalini will awaken all of the talents and gifts you have hidden inside of you. You will begin to use these talents for your good and the good of other people in your life. The Kundalini awakening will surge energy through your body and cleanse your soul of all of the things that are hampering your true potential.

You are the only person in the world who knows exactly how you feel. Other people might think they know the real you, or they might guess what you are thinking, but no one else will ever know for sure. You might be feeling boredom, pain, worry, or excitement, but if you hide it well enough, no one will ever know. When you begin your Kundalini awakening, you will no longer be able to hide behind a façade of fake feelings. During the awakening process, you will be forced to confront your inner emotions and all of the emotional baggage hidden in your life.

You might currently be highly successful in your life. You might have all of the material things you want or need, or at least everything you can think of right now. But having something does not mean you are successful or that you are living up to your fullest potential. While you have unfinished business with yourself, you will never be free, and if you are not genuinely free, you will not be truly successful. You will not know your true potential until you can be true to yourself.

Everyone is born with unlimited potential. The only restrictions on you and your prospect are the restrictions that have been put on you by the people in your life and the way you feel about yourself. Your personal opinion is often driven by other people's opinions and what they told you about yourself. During the Kundalini awakening, you will be forced to strip away all of the old experiences and events that you have kept hidden deep inside. These things are hampering your potential because, along with the old hurts and grievances, are the ideas that are making you fail. Every time you heard you weren't good enough, every time you weren't chosen for the team, every time you filed to succeed the way you thought you should, all of those old feelings are now keeping you from reaching the limits of your true potential. And the potential is nothing more than ability that lies dormant within you. It is all of the limited capability, hidden talents, unused success, and untapped strength that you can't reach because of all of the emotional baggage that stands in the way.
When you awaken your Kundalini energy, you will then be ready to awaken your potential. Once the transformation is complete, you will tap into life and inspiration from the universe and use it to help you reach your full potential. To understand your true potential, you need to understand the source of all life force, and you will achieve this understanding by awakening your Kundalini energy. You will have the ability to manifest your potential in reality with the power of the energy that flows through you.

You will see that your potential is equal to the assignment that you face. Maybe your mission is to make your workplace a happier place to be. Your potential to do that will equal your task to make everyone more comfortable. Your purpose gives you the responsibility to succeed, and that responsibility will make demands on your potential. After the Kundalini awakening, you will have the energy to accept the responsibilities that will awaken your true potential.

Awaken Your Divine Purpose

Kundalini is the spiritual energy that powers your consciousness. Your Kundalini lies dormant at the base of your spine until you begin the awakening. Then it starts to move upward through your body, through the chakras, activating them and bringing new levels of consciousness with every chakra it passes. When the Kundalini's energy reaches the upper chakras, it will reach the Third Eye Chakra and the Crown Chakra, which will allow for the full awakening of your spiritual self. You may suddenly feel electrified and ecstatic. These two chakras act like a magnet, pulling the energy of the Kundalini upward toward them. They are eager for the spiritual awakening that will come with the awakening of the Kundalini. Simultaneously, the spine's base has its magnet, which pulls the Kundalini energy back downward toward the unawareness, selfishness, and negativity that live in the soul before the awakening. Part of your spirit longs to return to the way things were before the awakening began, the amount of yourself that lived to serve only you.

During the Kundalini awakening, your ego will be stripped away to leave room for the spiritual side of you to emerge. When the energy is drawn away from the magnet of darkness at the base of your spine and brought fully to the attraction of light at the top of your body, true enlightenment will happen. This enlightenment is the point in your awakening when you realize your connection to the Divine and all the energy of the universe. Your real reason for existence is the relationship between you and the divine power in your life. You will need to desire spiritual experiences to be directly connected to you to experience self-realization.

Your Kundalini awakening will bring about your spiritual awakening. This transformation is your journey toward genuinely knowing yourself and all that lies within you. Before the awakening, you are trapped in service to your false self, your ego, the part of you that does not want things to change. Once you have stripped away the ego, you will achieve spiritual levels you never knew were possible. The old ideas that held you into a specific mold will be left behind in favor of the new freedom of higher thinking. You will realize that the pursuit of things will not bring you happiness, nor will they bring you closer to spirituality. Your spiritual self will take control when you are rid of your ego.

The spiritual awakening you will experience will give you the ability to move onto the next level of spiritual awareness. When you let go of the idea that your life needs to be defined by certain restrictions, you will begin to move to your spiritual awareness. You do not need a new identity because you already have one. You need to let go of what is not working in your life to let in what will help you succeed. Your thinking mind limits you in what you can know about yourself. Your spiritual self will bring the universe to you. You need to let go to achieve. You can't merely merge the new you with the old you.

When you give in to the new reality that your old ego needs to make room for the new spiritual you, only then will you be able to connect with the Divine and your spiritual self. This reality will allow you to live in the illuminating light of the Divine and enjoy all of the guidance, love, and compassion that the Divine will provide you. Your spiritual self will find it very easy to turn away from the darkness brought by the physical world. You can live in the physical world and still be a spiritual being. You will learn to let go of desires and attachments, and you will be able to see through the illusions and dramas before you. This awareness will allow you to find a higher path that will give you your true enlightenment.

Then you will live in the light of the universe, receiving all of the gifts it has for you. Once you connect with the Divine and realize your true spirituality, you will walk a new compassion and empathy path for others. Your intentions will be drawn away from material things and closer to spiritual things. You will turn your focus from the pull of the world and reach for the light flowing from the Divine.

CHAPTER 3
The Benefits Of Kundalini Energy

Awakening the Kundalini is the ultimate tool for improving yourself. It will allow you to realize positive changes that will last for the long term. When the energy of the Kundalini is awakened, it can't be held back. The awakening process is incredibly powerful. As the point moves through your body, you will feel intense feelings, and you will know you will never be the same again. Your unconscious thoughts will be brought out to become conscious thoughts or be eliminated. Everything will be brought forward, and nothing will ever be hidden also.

Personal Peace

Peace and serenity are often one of the motivations for people to awaken the Kundalini's energy inside themselves. Whether they consciously seek peace or just looking for something more in their lives, awakening the Kundalini will bring it. People spend a good part of their lives trying to feel better. Sometimes those good feelings come from questionable sources or destructive behaviors. But the goal is always the same.

With Kundalini awakening, you will cultivate your soul to be receptive to the peace in the universe around you. You will prepare your body to accept the vibrational level that will bring peace to you. Your awareness of peace will begin when your mind is neutral. Many people strive to gain inner peace through spiritual practice. Awakening the Kundalini inside, you will give you what you need to achieve inner peace. The stillness of inner peace is oneness with the universe. It is the space of witnessing the spirit used to observe the activities of the energy flowing through the body and the heart, body, and mind. This space is not restricted to time, and true stillness will not be separate from anything. No matter what experience you are having at the moment, peace will remain there always.

Inner peace is the collective response of the energy, heart, mind, and body to that stillness. The act of calm is a role model for your human self. The more attention you give to the silence within, the longer and deeper your mind, heart, and body will relax into inner peace. Awakening the Kundalini energy will leave you non-reactive to outside stimuli that once made you react negatively. You might still have periods after the awakening when you slip back into old habits when you allow your attention to become distracted, and you fall away from the stillness inside. When you react to events in the outside world, your inner peace will leave you, as the pattern of silence is broken. If this happens to you, turn your attention back to the stillness within. As you continue to do this, inner peace will become a more significant part of your life. This stillness is how you will learn to act and live from your space of inner peace. This peacefulness is how the outside world will affect you less.

The concept of inner peace is foreign to many people. For some people, it is just another form of relaxation. You will eventually realize that most of your prior experiences with ease were shallow than the depth of the inner peace you now have available. When you first begin your spiritual awakening, inner peace might be one of the first things you notice. You might feel a profound peacefulness washing over you. The light of the awakening will shine upon you as the clouds of darkness disappear. During the awakening process, you will encounter moments of the dark trying to return and obliterate the inner peace. As you progress further into your awakening, you will discover many long-buried emotions that you will need to deal with to get rid of. When this happens, the inner peace will disappear momentarily even as you try desperately to return to that peace. Your mind may consider these events to be a regular part of the daily routine, as you once accepted these events and did nothing about them. But doing that will prevent you from cleansing your emotional baggage and slipping into the inner stillness that is waiting for you.

As you learn to deal with your old emotions, it will be easier for you to turn back toward the inner peace you crave. It will require you to turn your attention back to the stillness and away from the turmoil. This retreat will make space for the spiritual growth that is emerging to continue your soul growth. Even after you have awakened your Kundalini energy and completed your transformation, there will be times when you will lose your focus on your inner stillness. Part of this is the fault of society that is always trying to drag your attention somewhere else. Giving your attention to your inner calm goes against everything you have been taught since birth. You will have a better understanding of how to mindfully engage with the outside world if you shift your attention to your inner, still every opportunity you have.

Focusing on your inner stillness does not mean shutting out or ignoring the external world. You will not be excluding your daily events, emotions, memories, and thoughts from your awareness. Inner stillness embraces all of you. Your ego excludes things, not your inner calm. Your ego will force away some memories and events to focus on others. It will repress or avoid certain emotions and thoughts while it tries to create new ones. The ego tries to avoid specific experiences in favor of others. This avoidance means that your ego is always trying to exclude part of you from your own life, and this will lead to suffering. When this happens, consciously turn your attention to your inner stillness. In the beginning, all of your thoughts and emotions will rise to the surface when you do this, trying to take over your attention. Work at having no response to these thoughts and feelings, but focus your attention on your inner stillness. As you focus on your inner calm, your inner peace will return. This ability will continue to become easier to do the more times you do it. Soon your everyday consciousness will create a union with your oneness.

As your ego fades away, your inner peace will strengthen and deepen. Your human self then will align to the stillness within. This openness will make you naturally more peaceful, and it will be easier to see any separation, illusion, or pain that still lurks inside your soul. Uniting your human self with inner stillness will never reject your life experiences. Instead, it will bring all pleasurable and painful experiences into its warmth and goodness. Then you will learn to get all aspects of your life into yourself so everything can take advantage of the inner stillness that will bring you inner peace.

Enhanced Psychic Ability

Just like you are born with the Kundalini energy lying dormant inside you, you are born with psychic abilities. Children have well-developed psychic skills. They do not know that they are not supposed to see, feel, or think. To a child, everything is real. As children grow older and the whole world steers them away from their psychic beliefs, they lose their psychic abilities. They accept the reality of the world around them and forget the knowledge they once had to see beyond reality and illusion. Since psychic power is never truly lost, just temporarily buried deep inside, it is easy to regain the ability during your Kundalini awakening.

Awakening your Kundalini energy will allow you to regain your psychic abilities. All of your spiritual gifts are hidden within you, but they are accessible to you. After your awakening, you will see that many of the things you have said or done were the hidden gifts you tried to avoid or ignore, or maybe you have been seeking to awaken these gifts once again. One of the spiritual gifts that are hidden inside of you is your psychic ability. If you have been trying to use your psychic abilities before your awakening, you probably misused them. For many people, the emergence of their psychic awareness requires spiritual healing and a new mindset.

Part of the world's truth that is amazing is that everything happens all at the same time. Time and place will merge into one illusion that will confuse your mind and your thoughts. As you travel through your awakening and allow yourself to be freer, place and time will become nothing more than concepts. When the awakening happens, you might become overwhelmed by the awareness and information that will suddenly burst forth. Because you have ignored your psychic abilities for so long, they will need some assistance emerging from the darkness where they are hiding. With your increased spiritual awareness, you will sense energy, see the future, and see and speak to spirits. Your psychic awareness will be another part of your existence.

The Kundalini awakening has turned on the light to illuminate your psychic abilities. Now that you can see all aspects of your life, you will see your psychic abilities once again. Once your psychic abilities have awakened, you will need to put some effort into using them so that they will be useful for you. One of the easiest methods of psychic ability to develop is clairvoyance.

The word clairvoyance means clear vision, and it is the ability to learn information about a location, person, event, or object by using extrasensory perception (ESP). With the capability of clear sight, you will see events or persons distant in time or space. Clairvoyance is three different abilities. There is precognition, which is the ability to predict or perceive future events, remote viewing, which is the perception of current events outside of the normal range of perception, and retrocognition, which can see events from the past.

Clairvoyant people see with their physical eyes and with their mind's eye. While both methods will work, the clairvoyant sees things with their mind's eye, their sixth sense. A clairvoyant can receive an image, but the real gift of clairvoyance lies in interpreting what the image means. Most people function better with some form of clairvoyant abilities. This ability enables them to read the vibes that other people emit and receive warnings from their spirit guides or other higher powers. You might already have clairvoyant abilities and not know it. If you think you have the gift of prophecy, you can display one or all particular skills. You might see flashes of images, symbols, numbers, colors, visions playing in your head like a scene in a movie, mental images that randomly flash before your eyes, or you might find it relatively easy to visualize or imagine events.

Flashes of light or color might be your spirit guide or your angels signaling you or sending messages to you. You might see random movements or twinkling lights out of the corner of your eye. Lights might flash or glitter in the air, or colored shapes or randomly floating orbs may appear. You might be able to detect others' aura that looks like a glowing orb that surrounds them. You might see shadows floating through the air around you. Visualization is a significant part of divination since it involves seeing things, either mentally or physically.

You will see in your mind how things work, you will know how to assemble something without using the directions, or you might have the inborn knowledge to fix small appliances because you instinctively know the problem. You will also have a marvelous sense of direction and rarely get lost, even when you are going to a new location for the first time. Any task that requires visual or spatial traits is easy for you. This power means you might excel at assembling puzzles, reading maps, or completing mazes. You prefer hobbies and jobs that allow you to use your creativity, and you possess a deep appreciation for beautiful things. If you have frequent vivid dreams or have a vivid imagination, you are probably a clairvoyant.

Increased Creativity

Awakening your Kundalini energy will awaken other abilities within you, and one of those is creativity. The Kundalini energy will draw you to forms of expression like film making, composing, photography, writing, and painting. Over time, the energy flowing through you will influence your brain, rejuvenating old information pathways, and triggering new ones. This will prepare your mind for excellent new means of expression in both the metaphysical and physical worlds. Having renewed creative ability just means your talent has been released from your subconscious. You will still need to work on your craft to improve. As long as you live in a physical body, you will be pulled and pushed by the arbitrary urges that your body subjects you to. Your creativity is your way to express yourself in the manner you want to express yourself. This expression is part of how you will confront the arbitrary urges of your body, so you have the power to define the journey of your soul through the Kundalini awakening. While working on your craft will improve your abilities, it is also important to step out of your comfort zone and experiment with your talent. Genius waits in the unknown world at the edge of your ability, as long as you will take that step into the abyss of the novel.

The Kundalini awakening will unlock energy channels in your body that will bring a more significant life force and vitality to your whole body. This flowing energy will have a marvelous effect on your heart and your brain. Creativity is driven by freedom of spirit, which leads you to a place of wild expression. You will enjoy an enhanced clarity of mind. An alive mind will help you remove society's restrictions and your own mind on your creativity and spirit. As the energy increases its flow, your imagination will turn from a trickle into a torrent.

Your awakening will connect you to the universe, a thing that is much larger than yourself and full of available energy. The cosmic force of the universe is the ultimate source of all creative power open to you. When you tap into the consciousness of the universe and experience yourself as more than just a body and an individual, you will then expand into a higher reality where your inspiration is waiting for you.

You will feel a marvelous sense of wellbeing after your Kundalini awakening. You will feel a palpable connection to something greater than you and the experience of the vital life force flowing through your body. Your expanded perspective will bring you visionary creations full of original ideas. It will help you be more open and receptive. Any of your egos that are left after the awakening will be softer. The mysteries of the universe will flow into you and drive your creativity because you are a receptive empty vessel, ready and waiting for divine inspiration.

Your spiritual, emotional, mental, and physical health needs to express yourself regularly by engaging in something creative. Creating things connects you to the divine energy that is within you. The idea is not to worry that you have no talent or you aren't good enough. You are not looking for perfection; you are looking for a creative outlet to release your expression. When you consciously engage your creativity, you are practicing being fully present at the moment, which is one of the purposes of awakening your Kundalini. Let yourself travel into the mysterious area where creativity is the journey and not the destination.

Better Spiritual Connections

Spirituality does not necessarily mean a connection to organized religion. It can be an attraction to a particular deity or just a belief in a higher power. It might be the reliance on an activity that makes you feel closer to your higher self. People who follow a religion or a particular practice are searching for a connection to their higher selves. This connection can easily be attained by awakening your Kundalini. As a conceptuality is challenging to define since most of the understanding of spirituality will depend on the person's perspective regarding spiritual matters.

Mysticism is a part of spirituality. All major religions feature some teaching of magic, which is how you will reach the inner dimensions of your life, a place where you will achieve your unity with the Divine Being of your choice. Spirituality is a concept with more possible meanings. It is sometimes associated with religious traditions that emphasize the growth of your inner spiritual life. This growth includes the ability to develop a spiritual experience that is deeper and more meaningful. Recently, the development of spirituality has moved farther away from the religious aspect and more toward achieving virtuous and ethical behavior as usual.

Mysticism in your everyday life means performing those activities based on faith while completing your regular daily activities. It is searching for and pursuing a relationship with some higher being. You desire a relationship that will bring spiritual truth to your everyday reality. The differences in social, psychological, and religious traditions will express how you define mysticism and spirituality. Beliefs like these are considered to be somewhere beyond the perceptual and intellectual mind. Mysticism is spiritual, but it is not spiritualism. Mysticism is an organic process that includes the perfect union with your Higher Power. The exact definition of mysticism will depend on the religious tradition that is defining it.

While mysticism has religious connotations, it is not reserved simply for religious people. The ability to understand mysticism is a trait you are born with, just like your spirituality buried deep inside until you resurrect it by awakening your Kundalini energy. You can perform different activities that will bring you closer to a union with your Higher Power. These activities include meditation, which will make you receptive to receiving messages from the Divine. Some people experience visions or voices because mysticism has been thrust upon them after a traumatic or unexpected experience. A traumatic experience is any experience that is outside of your normal realm of daily activities and not necessarily a negative one.

Spirituality is the solitary adventure that your soul takes as it seeks for morality and truth in your life. Spirituality shies away from worldly interests. And while spirituality is a broad term, it becomes even more comprehensive when defined by the different groups that seek spirituality. Native Americans, followers of the new age theory, monotheists, polytheists, and many others seek spirituality and determine what spirituality will be for them. In all groups, spirituality deals with developing the spirit as the master of your body.

You can only define the meaning of spirituality for yourself. The definition involves deeply personal subjective experiences. It includes being connected to power more extensive than you, and it affects your search for meaning in your life. As a human experience, spirituality is universal. You can describe your spirituality as being sacred if that is what it means to you personally. It will bring you a deep sense of being alive and connected to someone or something larger than you are. You can define spirituality in terms of your religious experience, but the act of being spiritual is more extensive than just being religious. While the two concepts are not the same thing, they are not that different, and they can overlap in your life. Spirituality will lead you to seek a better path for your personal life, more meaning in your life, and a way to feel connected to the universe and others. Mysticism will lead you to seek truth in life, the difference between right and wrong, and a desire to follow certain rituals that will bring you closer to your goal. These disciplines look for mental and emotional comfort, reflective thinking, the awe in ethics, and a belief in something that will watch over you and help you on your journey.

Additional Benefits to Awakening Your Kundalini

By channeling the dormant energy lying within you, you will awaken your Kundalini and connect with the power in the rest of the universe. This journey will transform your entire life. You will reap many benefits from awakening your Kundalini. These benefits might be answers to things you have been searching for, and they might be unexpected benefits you never knew were possible.

Cleansing— you will feel a sense of cleanliness and purification after a Kundalini awakening. When the energy is awakening, it will cleanse your chakras and your central channel as it pushes the life force to flow through your body. Since each of the chakras regulates the various psychological and physiological functions, cleansing them with Kundalini energy will also help cleanse and heal your physical and mental bodies.

Memory Improvements – awakening your Kundalini will clear out all of the stagnant material in your subconscious and your mind, so your powers of memory will significantly improve because of the cleansing it will receive during the awakening process.

Empathy and Compassion – activating your Kundalini energy will connect you to all creation and the universe. Once the power begins to flow, you will automatically feel more compassion for other people, and this will show in the level of empathy you extend to other people.

Deep Relaxation – this is one of the best benefits of awakening your Kundalini energy. You will be in an exalted state of bliss that you will never want to leave. Part of this is due to the increased supply of oxygen and blood that flows through your body along with the energy. All of the actions you take to awaken your Kundalini energy will unify you with the universe and all of the people in it. You will have total control over your mind. You will be in complete harmony with the universe and with yourself.

Aging Will Slow – the signs of aging like dark spots, dead skin, and wrinkles are all due to the stress of oxidation on the body, which causes damage to your cells. This stress is caused by inadequate oxygen supply, poor nutrition, mental and emotional stress, and pollution. One of the best benefits of awakening your Kundalini energy is the chance to combat aging signs by repairing the damage to the cells.

Magnetism – you will find that you are more attractive to other people due to your Kundalini awakening. Part of this is that you are now attracting the right kind of people in your life. You will attract those people who think like you do and see life the way you do. You will attract many good things into your life as you begin to radiate positive energy from your Kundalini awakening.

These benefits will begin to manifest in your life as soon as you start the process of awakening your Kundalini. They will not all be beneficial to you initially, but as the energy begins to flow through you, your excellent benefits will begin to shine through. If you are willing to put forth the effort needed to gain all of these benefits from awakening your Kundalini, you will be transformed on this fantastic journey that will connect you to all of the powers of the universe.

CHAPTER 4
Obstacles To Achieving Kundalini Energy

In awakening the Kundalini, the ultimate goal is to connect with the higher power through self-realization. Awakening your Kundalini will focus on raising your body's vibrational energy from the lower frequencies to the higher frequencies. This area is where you will be better able to connect with the Divine and the powers of the universe. As you walk your spiritual path to the awakening, you will move further away from your material reality and into your spiritual truth. But all of the techniques you use to awaken your Kundalini will be less than sufficient if your body, mind, and soul are not in an excellent place to receive the energy from the Divine. Awakening the Kundalini will cleanse your body, mind, and soul, but it will not work if those entities are not ready for the awakening.

Your spiritual journey requires your participation and your readiness to participate. In your quest to be liberated, you must be able to honor and accept your innate humanness as an essential part of merging your spirit with the Divine. This union will require that you be at one with Mother Nature, embrace your feelings and emotions, and care for your body. If all parts of you are not ready for the integration, your attempts to awaken your Kundalini energy will not be successful. In other words, you will need the purity of your body, mind, and soul. Purity means being free from anything that might contaminate you or impede your growth. Purity is complete and all-encompassing.

Besides ensuring that you are clean and pure, you will need to fully commit to the process of Kundalini awakening if you want to succeed in achieving self-realization. Achieving a union with the Divine is the highest purpose in your life. Some significant obstacles will prevent you from awakening your Kundalini and achieving real transformation to self-realization.

Ignorance – This is the inability to realize or be aware that you possess a divine, infinite aspect that can be awakened and enjoyed. You will need to honestly believe that you have the ability and the right to achieve Kundalini awakening before you can revive it fully. It isn't necessary to think that there is an eternal aspect of your life on earth. However, doing so and clinging to that belief is a valid technique that will lead you to enlightenment. You will need to consider that this is a possibility, and then you will need to explore your inner truth to see if you are seeking something eternal in this experience. If you reject the likelihood that you can be awakened with Kundalini energy, you will not reap the benefits of the awakening.

The process of self-realization will mean that you are entirely free from delusion. You will be able to express your real self and live in life entirely as you were always meant to live. If you only desire the pursuit of material pleasures instead of absolute enlightenment, you will not achieve Kundalini awakening. While there is nothing wrong with the quest for fame, power, wealth, or material gains, they can't be used as a substitute for true enlightenment if that is your goal. People often miss the point that the awakening of the Kundalini will allow you to live the life you deserve, and this will mean that you will be free to pursue those material items you desire. The difference will be that you will no longer attach such significance to these content items, so they will be easier to gain because you will not be quite desperate for success.

Impatience – You will be able to awaken your Kundalini if you want to, but the awakening will not happen overnight. It sometimes took years for students to learn the necessary skills from their masters to achieve self-realization in ancient traditions. Kundalini awakening and true self-realization is the highest achievement you will ever realize. In society today, instant gratification is the ultimate goal. Instant pleasure is essential.

This desire for instant gratification has also spilled over into the world of spiritual matters. Unfortunately, enlightenment will not happen instantly because it takes work and effort. You need to desire enlightenment and be willing to work for it. You will need to walk the path to self-realization for as long as it takes to achieve. The way to Kundalini awakening is often painful and can be stressful, but it will never be boring. Achieving full awakening will take time, but the reward you attain at the end will be worth the effort.

Laziness – Kundalini awakening requires work to achieve. The process is not for anyone who is not ready to put in the effort necessary to completely transform their lives. That is what a Kundalini awakening will do for you; it will completely change your life. Laziness has nothing to do with the energy that you put out in your life. Real laziness means being utterly unaware of yourself. Suppose you are aware of the actions you take and why you take them, the feelings that pass through you, and your thoughts as they happen, then you are not a lazy person. You are completely aware of yourself and your place in the universe.

You can be a very busy person and still be lazy. It helps if you were mindful of the moment and entirely in tune with yourself and the path you are walking. You will not achieve Kundalini awakening if you are not aware of yourself and your place in the world. During the awakening, you will go through many changes that you will need to be mindful of and ready to correct to move on to the next level.

Confusion – You can't be confused if you want to achieve true self-realization. The confused person is the person who has all of the material things they want or need, who knows that self-realization is the real purpose of life, and continues to pursue material gains. Instead of beginning the Kundalini awakening process, they continue to make excuses about why they can't start or can't succeed. These people are perplexed since they know what they need to do and still don't do what is required to awaken their Kundalini.

Everyone makes the mistake of being confused at some time or other in their life and sometimes more than once. You might neglect doing something you know you need to do because you don't want to do it. Sometimes life gets in the way temporarily, and everyone neglects their duties. But the confused people keep making excuses for why they can't begin their awakening or why they are not succeeding at their awakening. They are so confused that they lose sight that self-realization is the real purpose of life, which will only come with enlightenment. Awakening your Kundalini needs to be your one fundamental purpose in your life if you want to succeed at the awakening.

Compromising – Life and society will genuinely wear you down and take chunks out of your soul and heart. The young are full of vitality, fire, and attitude, and that slowly ebbs away, smothered by the difficulties of life and the endless responsibilities people have. It is never too late to begin your Kundalini awakening. You might feel you have waited too long, and it is too late for you to be successful, but it isn't. While you are alive, you will have the chance to succeed.

People will often make compromises with themselves. They tell themselves they will begin the process soon, just as soon as they can attend to whatever pressing concern is taking over their lives now. It is a compromise, and it does not work. The time will never be perfect to begin the awakening of your Kundalini. If you can take some time away from your responsibilities, in the beginning, to take care of yourself, then that is the ideal situation. But if you want this, stop making compromises and not wait any longer to get started on your Kundalini awakening.

Fear – As your time of awakening comes closer, you might begin to become aware of the true nature of your ego, and that awareness brings fear. It might feel like you are jumping off a cliff and risking the loss of everything. This feeling is the initial fear of surrender. You must be willing to surrender, to jump off that imaginary cliff that feels so real and risk losing the life you now live. You must be prepared to sacrifice everything. This sacrifice is why it takes great courage to awaken your Kundalini. And eventually, you have to do it. Surrender absolutely everything and jump off the cliff. Now is not the time for careful and cautious stages. Surrender is a bold move when the very nature of the separate self is fear. The individual ego of self-identity is created entirely out of fear, the fear of not surviving.

This spiritual death is what your ego is afraid of. The good news in all of this is that you will give up everything, you will surrender everything, you might lose everything, including yourself, and the result of all of this is that you will gain everything. You are only really offering your attachment to the worldly things in life, and that is nothing more than an illusion. What you will achieve is reality. You will gain the power of the world. You will gain relationships that were never possible before. You will gain peace. You will gain love. You will gain complete uninterrupted contentment full of joy and gratitude. You will gain freedom. You will gain life. And you will achieve your True Self.

Leaping is terrifying. Every person who has awakened their Kundalini has made this leap of faith. They have all experienced this terror. It is part of the nature of the awakening. The power of the transformation, the fulfillment of self-realization, makes everything worthwhile.

CHAPTER 5
The Ten Bodies Of Kundalini Yoga

Humans are very attached to their physical body. They identify with it and consider it to be the expression of who they are. You likely think of yourself in physical terms and rely significantly on your physical anatomy to enhance your potential. You might label yourself based on your physical appearance. You might even carry this definition of yourself like a private label. When you feel unwell, you try to heal the physical symptoms your body creates. That is a minimal way of thinking about your existence.

The teachings of Kundalini yoga point out that in addition to your physical anatomy, you also have more subtle and energetic structures to consider when you are trying to understand your strengths and imbalances and your existence. Those structures are your subtle anatomy, and they include your life force energy and the channels that it circulates through within your body. These structures also include your internal chakras system, which relates to your emotional, physical, and energetic capacities.

The Ten Bodies are the powerful capacities of your psyche, the conscious and unconscious parts of your mind. Each of your Ten Bodies has specific gifts that manifest when you are healthy and carry deficit tendencies that will surface when you are weak. The ancient teachers believed that all diseases existed first in one of these energetic spiritual bodies before manifesting outwardly. By learning about your Ten Bodies, you will understand where some of your imbalances lie. You will learn how to strengthen your weak bodies to make yourself naturally happier and healthier.

Your Soul Body is the First Body. The first one of your ten light bodies is your soul; your connection to the infinity within you. It is the foundation that connects you to your destiny and purpose. When your Soul Body feels balanced, you will feel the connection to your inner wisdom. Your intuition will be healthy, you will be creative, and your feelings will come from a place of understanding and humility. Your heart will rule over your head so you can relax and trust the flow of life. If your Soul Body is weak, you will react from your head instead of your heart. You will feel stagnant and stuck in place and unable to access your creative flow.

Your Negative Mind is your Second Body. This body is the area of your intellect that gives you discernment and will allow you to set personal boundaries. It will keep you alive, so while its name sounds negative, your Negative Mind is good for you. The Negative Mind is often your more substantial body, and it is continually working to assess situations for negativity or danger. A balanced Negative Mind warns you of potential hazards, keeps you safe and alive. It gives you the patience to hear your inner guidance. When your Negative Mind feels weak, you may fear the worst consequences and become overprotective and refuse to take action. You may choose to ignore the dangers of neglecting your better thoughts. If your Negative Mind is weak, it can cause you to take part in self-destructive relationships.

Your Positive Mind is your Third Body. This body will identify all possible opportunities and see the positive essence of all situations you might find yourself in. Your Positive Mind will encourage you and the willpower to take the steps necessary to reach your destiny. When your Positive Mind is balanced, you will have a good sense of humor and a clear understanding of hope. You will see the good in all and judge all situations with clarity and honesty. Your communication will be strong and direct. You will meet your challenges with strength and reverence. When your Positive Mind feels weak, you might ignore dangers or simply not consider the risks because you feel overly confident.

Your Neutral Mind is your Fourth Body. This body evaluates the information input from your Positive and the Negative minds and delivers guidance in a neutral form. Your Neutral Mind will align you with your destiny. When your Neutral Mind is balanced, it is meditative and will provide you with guidance from the viewpoint of intuition. It gives you the ability to see your polarities like right and wrong and good and evil. When your Neutral Mind feels weak, you will struggle to make decisions, obsessing over weighing every pros and cons. You might feel victimized by life because you don't know how to integrate your experiences and find your truth in them.

Your Physical Body is your Fifth Body. It forms the temple where the other bodies will meet. Your Physical Body allows you to balance yourself, experience life, and fulfill your desires. When your Physical Body feels balanced, you have the physical strength to go for your hopes and dreams and the willingness to sacrifice for them. You feel free to share your knowledge with others. When your Physical Body feels weak, you might be selfish and overly concerned with the perfection of your physical body. You may be jealous, greedy, angry, and competitive. There will be no balance in your realities and impressions.

Your Arcline is your Sixth Body. The Arcline is a line of energy extending across the top of your head from one ear to the other. Your Arcline holds the power you project and your inner radiance. It also acts as a protective shield. When your Arcline feels balanced, you can concentrate, focus, and meditate. The power you project is vital and helps you manifest your desires in life. You are less prone to experience negative thoughts and aggression. When your Arcline feels weak, you may be easily influenced by bad situations or unsavory people. You may be unable to manifest your desires because you are unfocused.

Your Aura is your Seventh Body. Your Aura is the field of electricity of energy that surrounds your Physical Body. Your Aura contains the power of your life force, and it is also a shield of protection. When your Aura feels balanced, it gives you a sense of presence and charisma. It elevates you to new heights mentally and spiritually. It will repel negativity and attract positivity. When your Aura feels weak, you may lack self-trust and be paranoid. The negativity surrounding you can penetrate your psyche and into your physical body, making you feel rundown and possibly ill.

Your Pranic Body is your Eighth Body. This body deals with your prana, the energy of life force that comes through your breath. Through your breath, your Pranic Body brings energy continuously into your system. When your Pranic Body feels balanced, and your breathing is relaxed and healthy, nothing will bother you. This body gives you the self-motivation and energy needed to take action and achieve your goals. When your Pranic Body feels weak, you might have chronic fatigue and constant low-level anxiety. You may feel defensive and fearful or try to get energy from food or stimulants.

Your Subtle Body is your Ninth Body. This body carries your away Soul when you die. It allows you to see beyond the immediate realities of life through the veil and beyond. When your Subtle Body feels balanced, you become stable and subtle. You have a powerful calmness and great finesse. You learn quickly and easily master new situations. When your Subtle Body feels weak, you might be naïve and easily fooled. You may be rough in your speech or behavior, or unintentionally crude. You may feel restless because you lack the peace that comes from flowing peacefully with life.

Your Radiant Body is your Tenth Body. This body gives you the courage and radiance you need to fulfill your destiny. It gives you the power to act despite feeling fear. When your Radiant Body feels balanced, you are radiant and charismatic. You exert an inspired respect and magnetic presence. You have real relationships with others, and your life is well-balanced and satisfying. When your Radiant Body feels weak, you might display an attitude of superiority, feeling that your way is the only way that exists. You might be afraid of conflict. You can shy away from the attention of other people, or you might feel ineffective and unable to rise to the situation.

When all Ten Bodies are balanced, you will reach full embodiment. This level is the Eleventh Body, the state you achieve when you are one with the Universe.

Kundalini Yoga balances and activates the Ten Bodies. Each position in Kundalini is a complete movement in itself. Keeping a regular practice is the best way to work on all Ten Bodies at one time. Suppose you feel an imbalance or weakness in one particular body, and you want to focus on strengthening and balancing that body in particular. In that case, you can do a meditation that will work that specific body, or which uses a mantra associated with supporting that aspect.

CHAPTER 6
Symptoms Of Kundalini Awakening

Your awakening process will be unique, entirely your own experience. With each awakening, there are common elements recognizable to all. The ravages of a Kundalini awakening are primarily physiological for some people. For others, the process is filled with emotional and mental torment. There might be some distress on both the psychological and physical levels. The symptoms differ in their degree of intensity and the length of duration for each person. Many people will experience only some material changes, while other people seem to encounter a full spectrum. The difference between Kundalini symptoms and other illnesses or disease is that the Kundalini awakening symptoms are continuously changing. New signs will appear as frequently as old ones will recede. The process of awakening is also limited because eventually, the symptoms will vanish. You might feel that something extraordinary is happening to you, even before you realize consciously that you are transforming. Many people are aware of the inner protection and guidance of an omniscient intelligence directing your process.

Rush of Energy
Kundalini will awaken and rise out of the central channel. The initial rising of the Kundalini is typically strong. Some people will feel energetic awakenings up their spine. Activation of your energy in the spine can be intense, and it can bring up experiences and emotions with every current of electrical sensations in your spine. Kundalini feels like a volcano is erupting up your spine, most especially the first few times it arises.

Kundalini is intelligent, and it will continuously cycle through stages of rising and receding. Depending on your awakening force, you might experience more severe physical, emotional, or spiritual symptoms. Kundalini energy is the source of all life energy. Inside you are a subtle power system that will nurture and protect your body, mind, and soul. You are born with this inner energy that will lie dormant until you take conscious steps to awaken it. This energy is perfect, pure, and indestructible. As it rises within you, the Kundalini energy follows its laws. It will also purify you, consuming and cleansing your imperfections. If you have ever felt the heat rising in your hands during your meditation, you feel the negative energy leaving your body.

Your body will experience physical changes during the transformation that may confuse you. The energies associated with spiritual awakening can cause some bizarre symptoms. The power of your Kundalini awakening will cause subtle changes in the receptors that you use for receiving and learning information.

Your senses may feel extra sensitive. You might begin to hear some things you never heard before the awakening. Colors might be more luminous and more vivid than you remember. Your fingertips will be ultrasensitive, and the things you touch will feel more intense than before, and the aromas you smell may seem overpowering. Your food will probably taste different, with the flavors being more intense. All of this is due to the energy of the Kundalini coursing through your body and awakening it in ways you have never felt before.

A Desire for Peace and Calm

As you begin to better connect to your true self, you will seek answers for your purpose in life. You might question anything you once took for granted. You might refocus your desires from the pursuit of money and fame to see those experiences with depth and meaning. You will alter your perspectives, and you will look for purpose in all things.

Inner peace is a deliberate state of spiritual calm that you will seek after your awakening. You will find this peace and tranquility despite the presence of external stress. You will enjoy a state where your mind will perform at an optimal level with a positive outcome. Peace of mind is generally associated with happiness, bliss, and contentment.

Peace of mind, serenity, and calmness are the feelings you will seek after your Kundalini awakening. The new energy of the life force will drive your inner peace and enlightenment as you continue on the path of knowing yourself.

This new inner spirituality might be difficult to embrace in the beginning because everyday stressors are still all around you. Finding peace and happiness in the joys of life might seem difficult at first, and results might not seem all that gratifying. Achieving true spirituality is a gradual process. With the energy of the Kundalini, you will find yourself becoming more spiritual every day.

Changes in Sleep Habits

A spiritual awakening will shift around a lot of stuff in your inner worlds. One notable change is how well you sleep. Sleep is one of the fundamental elements of life, and not getting enough sleep or not getting the right kind of sleep will directly impact how well you feel and how deeply you will experience life. Sleep issues will often underlie the problems of chronic fatigue that can also show up during your awakening.

Energy shifts and the healing process going on inside of you will utilize a lot of energy. Even when you are sleeping, you might be exhausted when you have done nothing significant physically. Your power shifts will come according to their timing and not your personal preference. This randomness can mean that they energize at night when you are ready to wind down. You might find yourself up late at night when you would rather be sleeping. You might be up all night long and then develop insomnia if your energy shifts' intensity is exceptionally high and unstopping. You might need to get up before you've had enough sleep depending on your schedule.

Never resist your transition even though the physical symptoms may be disturbing. Any resistance is you fighting with yourself, your truth, your love, and all of the essential things. This transition might not feel comfortable now, but later on, you will be grateful to be rid of all the illusions and pain that have kept you trapped your entire life. Sometimes simply embracing your spiritual awakening will allow you to sleep peacefully once again, but then you will spend your days processing and healing and growing spiritually.

The solution is to embrace your path. Do any spiritual work that you can during the day. Accept that you have changed and are still changing. The life you knew before is over. That life was an illusion, so it never really existed anyway. You were sharing a dream with many other people, which made your life seem safe, and it gave you things. But those things and that life were not real. Deep inside, you know this, and your soul knows it is time for this fantasy to come to an end.

Stronger Connection With Nature

Your natural affinity with nature is deeply rooted inside you. Connecting with nature is an emotional experience. When you connect with nature, you will feel close to the broader natural world. This relationship will help you feel good. Your response will help explain how being connected with nature is right for your health and well-being. Emotions are linked to your bodies' function, which includes your nervous system, heart, and brain. As the Kundalini courses' energy through your body, it will shape and direct what you do. Life's energy will drive you to seek a stronger connection with nature and the Universe around you.

The beauty of nature will calm your soul and help you channel your flowing energies. Beauty is a fundamental part of your lives. When you enjoy a more in-depth response when viewing beauty in nature, you will enjoy more overall peace. Noticing natural beauty will bring about well-being by promoting a stronger connection with nature, which is something your soul will crave after your Kundalini awakening.

Beauty comes from enjoying sensory experiences. After your awakening, the sights and sounds of the natural world flow in with ease. The beauty of nature brings pleasure that does not need to be useful. Beauty is fundamental to our relationship with the wider natural world as a simple sensory experience. The beauty of nature, along with the new energy of the life force flowing through you, is at the core of your unique connection to nature. Your physiological response to the beauty of nature will naturally intensify after your awakening.

Positivity Through a Positive Mind

The positive mind will see the good in every situation. It will keep the light shining vital no matter how dark things get. When your positive mind is critical, as the Kundalini energy flows through you, you will have a strong sense of hope. You will be full of bliss and joy, and you will be ready to succeed and take on life. Your positive mind corresponds to the seat of your will, so having a healthy, positive mind will lead you to be ready for this next stage of your life. Now that your positive mind is healthy, you will see all good that comes from the energy of the Universe and the energy of life that flows through you now.

When your positive mind is weak, it will find that the data from your subconscious is magnified. Negativity will discover your hidden traumas, blow them entirely out of proportion, and reinforce illusion and negativity. The emotions associated with positivity arc love, joy, and inspiration. You will possess this state of mind after your awakening, and you will choose good feelings and emotions. You will use the energy of the Kundalini to avoid damaging and unhappy feelings. Your thoughts are newly associated with positivity: feelings of self-esteem, courage, and certainty, and you will experience thoughts of love, peace, and happiness.

Embracing positivity does not mean ignoring your difficulties and bad experiences. It means you will acknowledge them, learn from them, improve yourself, and use the knowledge and energy you gain to embrace your new transformation.

With your new state of mind, while you might experience negative emotions and unpleasant experiences, you will not lose your spirit or your energy. Even when you hear negative stories and negative news, you will be able to climb above the ugliness in the world and not let negativity rule your life. You will have the strength to resist negative information, and you will refuse to let it take over your mind, your feelings, and your life.

Negativity awakens feelings of anger and fear, and these are powerful emotions. If you allow these emotions to arise in you, they will soon grow into huge issues that will affect your life and the lives of the people around you. Negative thoughts and emotions are contagious. You must resist them and stay positive. As you fill your day with positivity, optimism, and happy thoughts and feelings will fill your soul. You will desire to make your life better every day, and you will understand more what positivity entails and how to increase it in your life.

CHAPTER 7
Awakening Kundalini Through Your Chakras

Kundalini energy is the source of the force of life that is within you after the awakening. The power lies coiled against the base of your spine, where it had resided since before you were born. The energy is the inner fire of life that will flow through you after your Kundalini awakening. Once your Kundalini is awakened, it will rise in energy, much like liquid fire. When you activate your Kundalini's power, it will flow within you in the wavy shape of the serpent; this is used to represent it. The serpent curves upward from your spine's base into your gut and then past your heart and into your head.

The energy of Kundalini is known as Lady Shakti. She is the feminine half of the life in your body. She is the one who will activate the strength and the power in your body. Her goal is meeting with Lord Shiva, the masculine principle of consciousness, who resides in your Crown Chakra. Together Shakti and Shiva will manifest the full consciousness of the divine within you, transforming your life with the flowing energy of the Kundalini. Creation, movement, and action will join in the union when Shakti and Shiva unite. Shakti brings powerful energy that is aimless and disorganized. The power of the Kundalini will produce nothing by itself. It will require the direction and content of consciousness that will come from Lord Shiva. Without his leadership, energy and consciousness are nothing more than a dormant power incapable of any accomplishment.

Shiva's place in the Crown Chakra puts him at the highest of the seven internal chakras. Shiva holds the awareness of the universe and operates with freedom, purpose, understanding, and direction. Shiva is the vital union between the inner world inside you and the outer world you must live in, and his power will bring energy and strength to you. Shakti brings flexibility, along with her life and power. The goal of the Kundalini awakening is to bring Shakti to her meeting with Shiva. This meeting will unite the Root Chakra and the Crown Chakra and activate the chakras in between. Shakti rises when the Kundalini begins to awaken and brings her energy through the seven internal chakras, awakening and balancing them. She continues on her quest to the Crown Chakra and her desired meeting with Shiva. When the two unite, your Kundalini is awakened, and your energy will rise to transform you into a state of self-realization.

Awakening your Kundalini energy brings to you a power that many people seek because of the spiritual enlightenment it will bring. Kundalini energy is a powerful force that will fill your body with life as it courses through the channels in your subtle body. The point that the Kundalini awakening brings to you will never end. You will know a more substantial knowledge of your role in the universe and your goals in life. The Kundalini energy will bring you the power to seek wisdom and learning, bringing you strength. It is an infinite circle of power and energy. The experience will add clarity to your life, and the transparency will assist in the Kundalini awakening.

The energy from the Kundalini awakening will rise upward through your seven internal chakras as Shakti pursues her meeting with Shiva. Kundalini energy always follows and desires an upward path. As it travels, it will open and awaken your chakras as it passes through them. When the Kundalini's energy has opened your lower six chakras, it will complete its path to the Crown Chakra. There Lady Shakti will reunite with Lord Shiva. This merging will complete the circuit of energy that will give you the changes that you desire in your life. Then your subtle body will fill with conscious energy that is there for your use.

The Seven Chakras

To appreciate what they do for you, it is essential that you know and understand your twelve chakras. Having familiarity with the twelve chakras will significantly enhance your ability to heal and balance them. In the twelve-chakra system, five of the chakras are located outside of your body, and they are responsible for keeping you grounded to the earth while helping you receive energy from the universe. The other seven chakras are located in your body along your spinal column and up to the top of your head. Your lower chakras are physical, while the higher ones are spiritual chakras. The Heart Chakra is the meeting point for the two theories in your body, and it aligns with both the physical and spiritual aspects of the chakras.

Each of the chakras is aligned with a particular color, and the colors follow the spectrum of colors found in the rainbow, adding in gold and platinum. For the highest chakras, a combination of colors is referred to as iridescence or opalescence. Each chakra has a name and particular characteristics. Each of the chakras is aligned with a specific part of the body and controls that part of its health. Your chakras will work together to balance your body. Energy flows in them and through them to each other. The process contains all the energy that flows into and through your body. The color of the chakra is also found in the aura that surrounds your body. The intensity of these colors is directly affected by your overall health. A healthy, vibrant person will have an atmosphere that glows with bright, intense colors. The colors that represent unhealthy chakras will fade due to illness, stress, anger, or sadness.

THE ROOT CHAKRA – The Root Chakra is located at the base of your spine, and it is the center of your basic needs, security, and survival. The element of the Root Chakra is earth, and its theme is 'to be.' Your Root Chakra governs your legs, feet, and bowels. Your Crown Chakra balances your Root Chakra in your body. Red is the color that represents your Root Chakra since it is an entirely physical color. Red promotes the feelings of connection to the earth and being wholly grounded, so it works to keep you grounded physically and spiritually. Red will make you feel alert, vigilant, and primal. This chakra holds the foundation of the entire system of energy inside of your body. It is also the chakra that stores all of the excess energy for the other chakras. If your Root Chakra is blocked, closed, unhealthy, or spinning excessively, it will give off definite physical symptoms. Your physical problems could include your lower back, bladder, legs, feet, or colon. You might suffer from digestive issues such as irritable bowel syndrome. You can have weakness in your lower limbs, or you may feel ungrounded. You might be fearful, greedy, nervous, or possessive. You will probably entertain irrational fears about your safety, and you will likely have financial problems.

THE SACRAL CHAKRA -- Your second chakra holds the key to your most profound sensations and emotions. It will control how you express yourself and how you maintain your feelings inside your body. This chakra also controls your potential for creativity and the balance of light and darkness inside of you. Your Sacral Chakra is found deep within the lower part of your abdomen, under your belly button. Its corresponding color is orange, and its element is water. The theme of the Sacral Chakra is 'to feel,' and it corresponds to the bladder, hips, kidneys, lower back, and the reproductive system. Your Throat Chakra balances your Sacral Chakra. When your Sacral Chakra is unhealthy in any way, you will suffer illnesses of the bladder, kidneys, or the reproductive system. Your emotions will be unbalanced. You might feel confusion or shame over sexual matters or other intimate issues with your body, including harboring guilty feelings over those things you like to do. You might also suffer from various addictions since you will use these to make yourself feel better about yourself. Your Sacral Chakra is responsible for your sexuality and creativity. When your Sacral Chakra is healthy, you will feel friendly, passionate, and fulfilled. You will exude feelings of pleasure, joy, abundance, and wellness. When you feel free to express your creativity and love for your body, your Sacral Chakra will be healthy. A blocked Sacral Chakra will cause you to feel emotionally unstable or creatively uninspired. Your Sacral Chakra aligns with the color orange because this is the color of energy and creativity. The color orange gives people a sense of security and warmth—people associate orange with thoughts and feelings of pleasure, passion, and sexuality. Orange makes people feel abundant, sensual, and safe. You will need to maintain personal equilibrium while allowing creativity, happiness, and emotion to flow freely to keep your Sacral Chakra healthy. Your Sacral Chakra will grow stronger when you encourage a deep emotional connection with other people and a healthy, honest expression of yourself.

THE SOLAR PLEXUS CHAKRA – Inside the upper part of your abdomen, just behind your belly button, you will find your Solar Plexus Chakra. This area is where your inner fire begins and grows to ignite your self-confidence and willpower. Its theme is 'to do,' and the color yellow is associated with the Solar Plexus Chakra, and its element is fire. It aligns with your pancreas, liver, gallbladder, spleen, and stomach. Your Third Eye Chakra balances your Solar Plexus Chakra. If your Solar Plexus Chakra is unhealthy in any way, you will experience problems controlling your emotions, and you may have no willpower or self-control. You will either have low self-esteem or an exaggerated sense of your self-importance. You will alternate between feeling insecure and angry. You will struggle with gas, indigestion, bloating, fatigue, and weight control issues. If you are overly confident, you might have a protruding stomach that makes it appear that you are strutting when you walk. If you suffer from a lack of self-confidence, you will be seen walking and standing with rolled shoulders as you fold forward- looking timidly and defeated. The color yellow is an intensely emotional color. It will give you feelings of friendliness and confidence. Yellow will bring you thoughts and feelings of courage, self-esteem, and optimism. The color yellow will make you feel prepared, capable, and stimulated in the same way that a healthy Solar Plexus Chakra will. This chakra rules your self-esteem, balance, and action and focuses on your power, commitment, and individual willpower. It will govern all issues with your stomach, your digestive system, and your metabolism.

THE HEART CHAKRA – This chakra is centrally located in the center of your chest and is balanced by all the other chakras. It is the balancing chakra between the lower three physical chakras and the upper three spiritual chakras. Your Heart Chakra is the chakra that controls how you express caring and love for yourself and other people. Green is the color for your Heart Chakra, and its element is air. Your Heart Chakra aligns with your circulatory system and your lungs, arms, and heart. The theme of this chakra is 'to love.' An unhealthy Heart Chakra will cause your circulatory system, respiratory system, and possibly heart disease.

You will often feel co-dependent, jealous, lonely, and sad. You will sacrifice your desires to be able to take care of other people. You might also hold grudges against others because of that. Your Heart Chakra lies in your body's metaphysical and actual heart, and it is the center of the seven internal chakras. This chakra needs unconditional love to be able to function correctly. When your life is full of discord, when you have been betrayed by another, when you feel unrequited love for another, or grief is crushing you, then your Heart Chakra will be unbalanced and unhealthy. The color green will give you feelings of good health and well-being. It fuels thoughts and feelings of kindness, compassion, and love, and will make you feel healthy, alert, and empathetic. Your physical self and your spiritual self-come together in the Heart Chakra. This joining is where you will feel forgiveness, compassion, spiritual awareness, and love.

THE THROAT CHAKRA -- Your truths are honored and expressed in your Throat Chakra. Located in your throat, the Sacral Chakra is the balancing chakra. Its corresponding color is blue, and its element is ether. Your Throat Chakra aligns with your jaw, thyroid, shoulders, mouth, neck, and throat. Its theme is 'to speak.' If your Throat Chakra is unhealthy in any way, you might feel tightness or pain in your shoulders, jaw, or throat. Your thyroid gland may be diseased. You will either talk always or suffer through long periods of silence. You might find it challenging to speak your truth, and that lying is so much easier. You may have problems talking to other people or communicating your real feelings and thoughts. Your Throat Chakra is incredibly delicate, and excessively hearing other people tell you that your opinions are wrong or do not matter can damage this chakra. If your expression is suppressed, it can cause you to hide deep within yourself or close off all expression. Your Throat Chakra prefers open communication expressed with encouragement in a safe environment. The Throat Chakra will promote feelings of intelligence and trust. Feelings and thoughts of communication, logic, and duty go with the color blue. This color can easily make you feel more smart, well-spoken, and efficient. Your Throat Chakra is the first of the chakras that is an entirely spiritual chakra. An unhealthy Throat Chakra will cause you to have trouble speaking freely, staying focused, and paying attention when others talk. It may also cause you to fear being judged by other people. When this chakra is unhealthy, it can also cause physical ailments like problems with your thyroid gland, tension headaches, stiffness in your shoulders and neck, and excessive sore throats.

THE THIRD EYE CHAKRA – Deep knowledge and intuition lie in your Third Eye Chakra. This chakra is located directly in the center of your forehead. Its theme is 'to see.' Its corresponding color is indigo, and its unique element is light. This chakra controls your pituitary gland, the eyes, and the ears. The Solar Plexus Chakra is its balancing chakra. An unhealthy Third Eye Chakra will cause you to have trouble sleeping, which might include nightmares or night terrors. You might hallucinate or have other strange visions. You will most likely suffer from headaches and will often feel confused. Your sixth sense lies in your Third Eye Chakra, the reason that will allow you to determine your feelings about other people and situations.

When this chakra is unhealthy, you will feel disillusioned by life. You may think that your feelings and thoughts are not your own. To embrace your intuition, your Third Eye Chakra must be healthy and fully functioning. All things that will pass between the outside world and you must go through this chakra because it is the bridge between you and the outside world. An opened Third Eye Chakra will allow you to see what is real even if it is clouded by illusion and drama. If this chakra is unhealthy, you will find it difficult to use your intuition, learn new skills, recall important facts, or even trust your inner voice. When the lower chakras are imbalanced, it will make the Third Eye Chakra imbalance and make you feel more introverted, judgmental, and dismissive toward other people. It can cause you to feel anxious, depressed, and suffer from headaches and dizziness.

THE CROWN CHAKRA – The highest of the chakras inside of your body is the Crown Chakra. It is where the divine entity's source is found, and it is your connection to the spiritual world beyond you. This chakra rests on the top of your head. Its color is white or violet, and no element corresponds with it. The Crown Chakra directly controls your cerebral cortex, responsible for personality and intelligence, gross motor skills and adequate motor function, processing language, and the operation of your senses and your pineal gland, which is responsible for the regulation of all of the hormones in the body. Its theme is 'to understand,'

and the Root Chakra balances it. If your Crown Chakra is unhealthy in any way, you will have problems with your spirituality. You may deny the existence of any sort of higher power. You may become overly opinionated or feel as though you do not connect well with other people. You will probably struggle to understand spiritual concepts, and you might even fear anything that has to do with spirituality and mysticism, such as the occult or religion. You will have no access to your higher powers if your Crown Chakra is not healthy. This can cause you to feel isolated or emotionally distressed. The colors of the Crown Chakra, violet and white, stand for oneness, spirituality, and meditation, as these are the ways to gain access to the powers of your Crown Chakra. Living with an unhealthy Crown Chakra is possible, but you will never feel genuinely spiritual or one with the universe.

The energy of the Kundalini must rise past your internal chakras on its path to awakening. The chakras can't remain blocked if the Kundalini rises to its quest of your Crown Chakra. The Kundalini and the chakras will need to work together so you may experience true self-realization. By opening your chakras, you will facilitate the flow of healing energy up the central channel to aid in your transformation.

CHAPTER 8
How To Awaken The Kundalini

You will release the energy of the Kundalini and all of the power that will bring to you when you awaken your Kundalini. This energy will merge your subconscious with your consciousness when your mind is free. This freedom from thinking is the path to true enlightenment. You will open your spiritual channel of oneness and erase all illusion and duality from your life. Duality is the act of seeing yourself as an entity separate from the universe, man, and nature. When Shakti and Shiva join your Crown Chakra, there can be no duality because their union will bring you spiritual awakening and awareness. This energy will lead you down the correct path to happiness, and it is not conditional. It will never demand that your life follows a definite direction. You will finally be one with all of creation. Your transformation will bring you to the exalted state that you seek from your Kundalini awakening. You will become part of everything and everyone. You will finally possess in-depth knowledge and higher levels of energy, both physical and spiritual.

Ancient students of Kundalini learned how to understand the Kundalini's basic ideas before knowing any of the methods needed for awakening the Kundalini. This method was meant to make sure the students understood the procedures and the possible results before attempting the awakening. The primary objective was to release the full potential of human awareness from within. You will recognize your understanding, expand and refine your attention, and use your new awareness to achieve your unlimited self. As you clear out your inner duality, cultivate your inner peace and tranquility, create the ability to listen deeply and understand fully, and maintain a level of excellence in all that you do in life.

Meditation and Breathing
Kundalini yoga meditation is nothing more than a simple technique designed to use the power that you already possess in your mind, body, and senses. You will use these powers to create communication between your body, your mind, and your soul. You will learn to practice meditation so that you can spend time with yourself in a relaxed atmosphere. This time of reflection is your time to talk to your higher self, to connect with your breathing, to establish your rhythm, to acknowledge and enjoy the life force within your body, and time to become

more in love with your unique life circumstances. Meditation is your choice to spend time with you.

Using daily meditation will cleanse your mind like you use a shower to cleanse your body. This time is your opportunity to remain entirely in the present and clear out your subconscious. Meditation will teach you to be kinder to others, healthier, and more able to avoid mistakes in your life and higher energy levels. It will allow you access to the opportunity to create calmness and tranquility within your mind that will help you avoid reacting unfavorably to the constant flow of thoughts from your mind. You will have time to process your feelings and thoughts comfortably while you relax and revive your mind and body. This rejuvenation period will allow you to create a better rapport with the people around you and help you handle stress more efficiently.

Any time you feel alert is a perfect time to meditate. Some people meditate early in the morning when the world is peaceful. Others find meditating just before going to bed at night will help to clear their minds of the events of the day. You should not meditate right after consuming a large meal since your body will be preoccupied with digestion, but other than that recommendation, there is no best time to meditate. The length of your meditation is also your decision. Every meditation will work on a different part of your body or mind, and every meditation will be different. Begin with a limit on your time that will suit your needs. You will need to be comfortable with all aspects of your meditation, or you will have no desire to remain faithful to your practice. Meditation will allow you the opportunity to spend a few minutes in quiet relaxation—dress in whatever clothing you feel is comfortable for you. When choosing clothing, you might want to think about following the ancient practitioners' manners who considered meditation to be their special time. They chose clean, fresh, lightweight clothing that was usually white. They often liked to cover their heads with a prayer shawl or a turban.

Meditations will also use your breathing in different ways. You might break your breath into small segments while chanting a mantra. You might choose a specific breath pattern that regulates your inhales and exhales. You might simply focus your attention on the flowing depth of your breath. Your energy levels and moods are directly related to breathing, so altering your breath pattern or the rate and depth of your breathing will also change your mood and energy.

There is an easy meditation that will help to awaken your Kundalini energy that you can use to begin your practice. Sit comfortably with your spine straight but not stiff. If you are sitting on a piece of furniture, do not let your back touch the furniture, but keep your pose more upright. Put your feet softly flat on the floor and keep them relaxed. Put your hands in your lap, with the left one underneath the right one. Lower your eyelids until your eyes look almost closed, but allow just a thin line of light to filter in. Lift your chest to support your spine but relax your shoulders and neck. Focus your entire attention on the flow of your breath while you breathe in and out through your nose only. Do nothing other than noticing your breath and see how it moves in and out of your chest and how your body reacts to airflow. Consciously slow your rate of breathing after focusing for a few minutes. Normal breathing is fourteen to seventeen inhales and exhales each minute, so try to slow your breathing to eight cycles per minute. Listen closely to the sound of your breath as it flows in and out.

For correct Kundalini meditation and yoga, proper breathing is vital. Your practice will help you cultivate your breath's awareness and help you integrate appropriate breathing into your daily activities. The effects of your powerful breathing will significantly enhance yoga poses and meditation. You will detoxify your body, release irritability and insecurity, improve your digestion, cleanse your aura, balance the two sides of your brain, strengthen your nervous system, and clear your mind while it oxygenates your entire body. Proper breathing will also help balance your energy with your life force.

Several breathing techniques are an essential part of Kundalini yoga, and you need to do them correctly to enhance your yoga practice. These techniques are used along with specific postures and movements to create powerful effects in your body. Alternate nostril breathing will take advantage of your ability to breathe through either your right nostril or your left nostril instead of using both nostrils at one time. Correct nostril breathing will energize you and alleviate unbalanced emotional and mental states and irritation or depression. Left nostril breathing activates your lunar energy and helps you be more patient and learn to let go. You will do left nostril breathing to calm your nerves and mind and to help you relax. Use this breathing right before bedtime. To do either right nostril or left nostril breathing, simply block the other nostril with your thumb or finger and exhale and inhale long and deeply through the other nostril. You can also do alternate nostril breathing to create a balanced state that is both energizing and relaxing. Breathe in and out through one nostril first, and then the other.

The amount of heat needed to stimulate and awaken the Kundalini energy is known as the Breath of Fire. It activates your capacity to be centered in your body and your ability to focus. It will also nurture and energize all of the systems in your body and oxygenate your blood. Breath of Fire needs to be performed correctly for it to work correctly. When you exhale, pull your belly button in toward your spine. The belly button will automatically relax and go back out in the inhale. Focus on short inhales and exhales and let the inhale enter automatically; only the exhale is forced. Breath of Fire is a light, rhythmic, and relaxed type of special breathing. Do not consciously engage your abdominal muscles because this will make your breath heavy and slow. Do not use or tense your muscles in your face, shoulders, or chest, and make sure your ribcage stays relaxed.

One common mistake that many beginners will make when doing Breath of Fire is to inhale forcefully. If you do this, you will slow your breathing because only the exhale is supposed to be active. The exhale and the inhale need to be the same length, but you will allow the inhale to happen by itself. You will know when you are not doing the Breath of Fire breathing correctly because your entire upper body will tense up. The first breath will need to be drawn long and deeply, to make you aware of how your body moves when you breathe. When you first begin Breath of Fire, do just a few and then stop. This trial will let you feel exactly how it is done without allowing the breath suffering.

Long deep breathing will allow your energy and your breath to flow freely. To properly do this technique, you will need to keep your spine straight. You have three zones of stretch in your spine, and these correspond directly to the three sets of muscles that will move when you inhale and exhale. You will facilitate deep breathing when you stretch and strengthen your spine in these three areas. To extend your muscles from the bottom of your ribs to your base, pull your belly button in a little bit toward your spine to make your pelvis tilt forward. Do not lean forward so that your posture will be more upright. Sitting directly on your bottom instead of leaning forward will facilitate your grounding with the earth as you will connect more solidly with the floor under you. This position will also free your stomach muscles to make them better able to do long periods of deep breathing. Your muscles that surround your rib cage will need to be healthy and well-developed by raising them with your breathing. The smaller muscles stretched over your diaphragm will then extend your breath so that you can reach your maximum inhale.

People sometimes will cut off their exhales prematurely and then initiate inhaling by using the small muscles in their upper chest instead of their diaphragm muscles. You do not need to push the inhale to get proper air intakes. You will only need to exhale if you are taking in a deep inhale entirely. Before you begin your breathing practice, spend a few minutes simply observing your breath, to see if you are putting more force on your inhale or exhale. With careful training, your diaphragm will automatically work to produce exhales and inhales, your diaphragm will grow more robust, and your exhalations and inhalations will lengthen significantly. This breathing technique will also help improve the quality of your voice and your vocal capacity.

Breath suspension is a useful technique for holding your breath while you are doing yoga poses. Suspending your breath will mean relaxing the muscles in your ribs, abdomen, and diaphragm. This technique will help you support a profound internal self-transformation. You will stop breathing on your inhale by first inhaling deeply, lifting your ribs slightly, and relaxing your face, throat, and shoulders. Pull your chin in a little bit, and then sit calmly and still. If you feel an overwhelming urge to exhale, try just letting out a bit of air to relieve the pressure. You can also suspend your breathing on your exhale by completely exhaling first, and then pulling your belly button back toward your spine. Lift your lower chest area and then let your upper chest relax. If you ever feel the urge to inhale, try to exhale a bit more. This technique will teach your body how to extend the suspension without struggling or straining for air.

When you suspend your breathing, you will gradually recondition your central nervous system. When you stop breathing on the inhale, it can temporarily increase your blood pressure, and suspending your breathing on the exhale will temporarily lower your blood pressure. When you stop your breathing, you impact the sympathetic and parasympathetic parts of your central nervous system. These parts of your nervous system will activate during a perceived danger and then calm your body, respectively. Your brain will know how to trigger inhaling when your carbon dioxide level in your blood is too high, which is what the brain responds to and not your oxygen levels. You can get ready to suspend your breath by taking several long intakes of air and then exhaling completely to rid your body of any excess carbon dioxide. It will take patience and regular attention to build your practice. If you ever feel dizzy or disoriented, immediately stop, because this is not a sign of enlightenment. Your body will not help you if you push your body too far beyond the limits of its natural capacity.

Passive awareness breathing might seem like a simple exercise, but it is an essential step on the journey to true enlightenment. Observing the act of your breathing and how it flows in and out of your body will keep you calm and bring you back to the center. For real passive awareness, you will need to be aware of your breath as it rushes through your body. Imagine that your breath is flowing into your lungs, which part of it is going up to distribute itself in your head and around your brain. More of your breath will flow sideways, flowing out into your arms and hands. The rest of the breath will flow downward, into your legs and down into your feet, coming back up to rejoin the rest of that breath so that all of it can leave your body on the next inhale. This method is called passive awareness of your breath, using your mind to follow your breath through your body by calmly observing its path.

The one-minute breath method is an excellent technique for calming your mind and body. It will help you feel more open to the divine spirit. You will develop better intuition, and your physical brain will work better and more efficiently. Most people will take between fourteen and seventeen inhales and exhales every minute. Someone who has practiced breathing techniques might get that number down as low as eight breathing cycles per minute, and a well-trained yoga guru will breathe in just four breath cycles each minute. With the one-minute breathing technique, you will learn to take only one breath each minute. You will inhale for twenty seconds, hold that inhale for twenty seconds, and then exhale the breath for twenty seconds. Do not try to do the whole twenty-second cycle on the first try, as you may need time to build up to this level. Try doing just five or ten seconds if you need to, and work up to the twenty-second cycles. When you can do it completely, you will feel the immediate benefits that it provides. You will be able to calm down more quickly and enter a state correctly for meditation more quickly. If you can master this breathing method, you will be able to master every aspect of your spiritual and physical condition.

Crystal Therapy

Besides the central channel through which the Kundalini energy rises, other channels allow the Kundalini's strength to flow through in your body that are known as meridians. These channels are responsible for allowing the power of your life force to flow where it is needed the most. The meridians are all connected, so a blockage in one area of your body can be felt in another place. These blockages can be handled effectively by using crystals. A block will often appear as an ailment or a physical illness.

When you are awakening the energy of your Kundalini, and all of your attempts have been unsuccessful, the reason might be due to one or more of your seven internal chakras being blocked. When this happens, the Kundalini's energy will not be able to access your top chakra, your Crown Chakra. Crystals are a fantastic tool for opening your chakras and eliminating the blockages that keep your energy from flowing freely through your central channel and the meridians. You can do this using just one crystal or a crystal in colors to match every chakra.

Your chakras rest along your central channel, and they connect your mind and body to your emotions and your spirit. If your chakras are blocked, you will experience your mind, soul, and body issues and illnesses. Your chakras can become blocked for many different reasons, including diseases, emotional upsets, or problems with your karma. Even cases with their origin in your past lives or childhood events can cause blockages in your chakras. Using crystals that will vibrate at the optimal frequency for each chakra will work to balance and align all of your chakras.

The easiest method to align all of the chakras at one time is to lie down and set a crystal on each of your chakras. You can choose a crystal that is associated with that particular chakra and its corresponding color as the following list shows:

- Root Chakra – Smoky quartz crystal -- black or red crystal
- Sacral Chakra – Carnelian crystal -- orange crystal
- Solar Plexus Chakra – Citrine crystal -- yellow or gold crystal
- Heart Chakra – Rose quartz crystal -- green or pink crystal
- Throat Chakra – Chalcedony crystal – blue or indigo crystal
- Third Eye Chakra – Amethyst crystal -- violet or purple crystal
- Crown Chakra – Clear quartz crystal -- white or clear crystal

The process for cleansing your chakras will require you to lie still and relax for a minimum of ten minutes with the chosen crystal in place over your chakra that it corresponds to. Focus on making your breathing deep and steady, and meditate if you feel the need. So you would place the Root Chakra crystal just beneath the Root Chakra, somewhere near the tops of your legs or right between them, and the crystal for the Crown Chakra will be put on the top of your head. Put the remaining crystals on your body at the place where the corresponding chakra is located in your body. Clean the crystals well after using them so they will be ready for the next usage.

You might not always have the perfect crystal or even a crystal in every color for every chakra. If all you can manage is two crystal pieces to open your chakras, those two will be enough, as long as you are using clear quartz crystals. This particular crystal carries the characteristics of every other crystal in the universe. A piece of quartz that is clear can be used in place of any crystal for any application. Since the crystals are multi-use crystals, they will need to be programmed for the purpose you want to use them for. After using an approved method for cleansing your crystals, hold them in your hands, and repeat your intention. Then lie down, place one crystal near your Root Chakra and one crystal near your Crown Chakra, and follow the method outlined above.

Another method that works is the Crystal Point Method. For this method, you simply need a crystal point. This point is a piece of clear quartz flat on one side and pointed on the opposite end. You will first need to cleanse the crystal. Then lie down on your back and hold the crystal in your non-dominant hand with the point showing. Begin at the Crown Chakra and make nine circles that spiral outward. The crystal point will move in the same direction as the clock moves while it hovers over the Crown Chakra. Then move your hand down to the Third Eye Chakra and draw a line back and forth from the Third Eye Chakra to the Crown Chakra by moving the crystal down, then back up, and then back down. Then repeat the clockwise circles over the Third Eye Chakra, rotating the crystal held in your hand nine times. Next, return your hand up the line to the Crown Chakra and follow the line up and down several times. Now follow a line down from your Crown Chakra to your Third Eye Chakra and then down to your Throat Chakra. Move the crystal up and down from the area of the Throat Chakra near to your Third Eye Chakra and then to your Crown Chakra, then return to the Throat Chakra and make the nine concentric circles.

Repeat this process for each chakra until you reach your Root Chakra. Always make the nine concentric circles, always moving in an outward spiral, always returning to your Crown Chakra to bring the energy down along the line of your chakras to the next chakra that is in line until all of the chakras have been balanced, all the way down to the Root Chakra. After reaching and completing the Root Chakra, lie still for a few minutes and mentally visualize the energy flowing from the Crown Chakra down to the Root Chakra and back up the line to the Crown Chakra. Always cleanse the crystal after using it.

Using your healing crystals to unblock your chakras will allow your Kundalini energy to flow freely through your central channel and then to your physical body through your meridians. The crystals' vibration will also work with the life in your body to promote heightened spiritual enlightenment and spiritual, emotional, mental, and physical healing.

Kundalini Yoga

Kundalini yoga is a vibrant blend of physical and spiritual practices that incorporate meditation, breathing techniques, movement, and chanting mantras to achieve spiritual enlightenment. You will learn to build an increased level of consciousness and physical vitality. Your natural strength and stamina will unfold and grow during your practice of Kundalini yoga. It will help you shed the old you in favor of the new, more enlightened you. Your ultimate goal will be to unblock your chakras and silence your mind so you can increase your awareness of self. Kundalini yoga is the ancient art that mixes different practices to expand your consciousness. You will use the poses (asanas) along with chanting the sacred sounds (mantras), the breathing techniques (pranayama), with the cosmic energy (prana) to open your seven internal chakras and allow the strength of your Kundalini to flow upward unimpeded. As your practice begins to deepen, you will learn to unite your body with your cosmic consciousness and help direct your energy flow where it is needed most in your body.

All forms of life that you interact with are filled with energy. The practice of Kundalini yoga will awaken you to the power of your internal energy. It will guide you through the ups and downs in your life by helping you be calm in all situations. In the early days of its creation, Kundalini yoga studied the spiritual philosophy and the science of energy. It was taught to the students of Kundalini by trained masters. The masters would spend years reciting their spiritual visions to the students before they were allowed to progress further in their training. When Kundalini was brought to the Western world, all teaching facets became available to all people.

Kundalini energy is a tool you will use to achieve a life full of endless love along with lightness, joy, and inner peace. Your yoga practice will make you more aware of your body and how your Kundalini energy will affect your emotions and thoughts. You will have places in your body where your energy has stalled, locked areas that prevent the power of the energy from flowing freely, and these will interrupt the connection between your mind and body. These blocks will also prevent you from connecting with your higher potential and the universe around you. Kundalini yoga will cause the energy at the base of your spine to travel upward so your energy will flow, and your chakras will balance and open.

Kundalini yoga will help you build physical strength in your whole body. Each of the individual poses is held for an extended amount of time, sometimes for up to five minutes, so practicing this yoga is an excellent way for you to tone and strengthen your muscles. It is especially beneficial for building core muscle strength since many poses are done with specific breathing methods. Regularly practicing Kundalini yoga will help release the same hormones in your body that strenuous exercise will. Your moods will be improved by removing the hormone serotonin, also known as the happy hormone. The release of other hormones, along with the deep breathing techniques, will help you to lower your blood pressure. The extended, deep, slow breathing techniques of Kundalini yoga will reduce your stress and relax your nervous system. Cognitive function is majorly impacted by the lowered stress levels and the release of beneficial hormones, boosting your memory and concentration. Since your core and muscles around the diaphragm are strengthened, Kundalini yoga will help you improve your digestion and speed up your metabolism.

While all yoga sessions are different, each one will usually follow the same basic elemental composition. You will start with an opening chant designed to warm and tune your body. Then the kriyas will be performed. A kriya is a pose or a posture that is linked with a specific breathing technique. After all of the poses are complete, there will be a closing meditation of some sort. Teachers and students alike will often wear all white clothing or light in color because white is considered to extend your aura and ward off any negative energy. Kundalini yoga is a more spiritual practice compared to other forms of yoga. As your power begins to awaken, you will find that you are spiritually connected with the universe and yourself. You will experience internal peace, along with increased energy, creativity, charisma, and empathy.

The Lotus Pose is a right beginner pose for those wanting to try Kundalini yoga. It is a basic pose that is done while you are seated that helps to open your hips. This pose is a good posture for those who need to relieve tightness in the hip area but check with your doctor if you have any current hip issues. Sit on your floor and extend your legs out in front of your body. Keep your spine erect but relaxed. Get into a cross-legged position with your feet near your body and your knees pointing outward. If you can, cross your legs to put the left foot on top of your right thigh and vice versa. Sit and meditate as long as you are comfortable in this position.

The Cobra Pose is an essential pose for awakening your Kundalini energy. Place your body flat on the floor on your stomach, with your feet and legs pressed firmly together. Rest the tops of your feet on the floor. Set your palms of your hands firmly on the floor under your shoulders and push your upper body up to your waist. Keep your arms straight, and your shoulders and neck relaxed but upright. Hold this position for at least thirty seconds, longer if you can, and breathe deeply and evenly the entire time.

The Archer Pose works to make you feel strong and confident like a warrior. Stand upright with your spine straight but not stiff and your feet close together. Turn out with your right foot, so it is resting at a forty-five-degree angle to your left foot. Step back with your right foot, straightening your leg while keeping your foot turned outward. Bend your left knee at a ninety-degree angle. Never let your knee extend out beyond your toes. Lift your hands to the level of your shoulders while you keep your arms straight. Put your hands into loose fists with your thumbs pointing at the sky. Turn all of your upper body to the left and place your right hand on your left side just below the armpit. Hold still in this position for several minutes, and then repeat the sequence on the right side.

In other kinds of yoga, the poses flow with the breath, while in Kundalini yoga, the poses are combined with chanting and breathing. The purpose of this is to promote extended spiritual enlightenment, which makes the practice of Kundalini yoga a more spiritual form of yoga.

Oils and Aromas

Essential oils are the distilled essences of the fragrance of different plants. They can be used to remove blockages in your chakras so that your Kundalini energy can flow freely through the central channel. If you are using this method, you must choose the scents that you like. The essential oil will not work if you do not want the smell, and you either refuse to use it or do not believe in its power.

When you are using essential oils on your skin, you will need to use a carrier oil, which the essential oil is mixed with. Essential oil is too concentrated for you to put it directly on your skin without a carrier oil. Choose from your preferred carrier oil such as almond, avocado, jojoba, olive, or coconut. Mix a few drops of the essential oil into the carrier oil and rub it on your skin over the chakra that needs unblocking.

Another method is to rub your palms with the essential oil of choice and then wave your hands through the air to disperse the scent through the air around you.

You can also treat your environment by using an oil diffuser. This item is a small glass or ceramic bowl or vase-shaped object with a smaller neck and a wider bottom. There is a space underneath for a small candle to rest. Simply pour a bit of the essential oil into the bowl and then light a tea light candle underneath. As the candle warms the bowl, it will allow the fumes of the essential oil to escape into your room. Each of the chakras has specific scents that work best with that chakra:

- Root Chakra –myrrh, rosemary, frankincense, patchouli, sandalwood, clematis, and ylang-ylang

- Sacral Chakra – hibiscus, jasmine, orange, rose, and lady's slipper

- Solar Plexus Chakra – peppermint, juniper, yarrow, chamomile, vetivert, and marjoram

- Heart Chakra – rosewood, holly, poppy, rose, bergamot, jasmine, pine, and eucalyptus

- Throat Chakra – chamomile, sage, cosmos, trumpet vine, lemongrass, geranium, and hyssop

- Third Eye Chakra – frankincense, patchouli, lavender, spruce, clary sage, rosemary, wild oat, peppermint, and Queen Anne's lace

- Crown Chakra – myrrh, jasmine, lotus, frankincense, sandalwood, star tulip, neroli, benzoin, and lavender

CHAPTER 9
Life With Kundalini Energy

Once you have awakened your Kundalini energy and it is flowing freely through your body, you will be the recipient of so much more spiritual and emotional range than you ever thought possible. Releasing the Kundalini energy will provide you with access to powers that you may have only dreamed of before.

Intuition

Having intuition refers to having a form of knowledge that appears to you without conscious thought or apparent deliberation. Instinct is not magic. It is a process by which the unconscious mind will develop an idea based on past experiences and the person's accumulated knowledge. People with intuition are not aware that the process is working or how it works, but they know when they have feelings. The brain can register the information without the conscious knowledge of the individual.

It is believed that intuition relies heavily on the powers of matching patterns of thought in the way that the mind searches its stored experiences looking for situations that are similar to the one the individual is currently facing. The process that underlies intuition can present judgments in mere moments. Like first impressions, intuition is the brain's need to predict what will happen next and prepare for it to happen. People form first impressions of other people based on the rapidly developed holistic assessments of them. These impressions are based on the judgment of the cues the brain intercepts that might lead to harm or help.

Intuition, or gut feelings, does play a role in making complex decisions. Intuition is frequently used as the reason for an individual acting in a particular manner. And most people will not readily admit to the fact that they made their decision based on a feeling. Even though intuition plays a large part in most individuals' everyday lives, it is still challenging to try to define it. Almost everyone experiences intuitions, that feeling in the gut, from time to time. It is that unconscious feeling that you must perform a specific action without knowing why you must accomplish that act. People who are completely in touch with their sense of intuition have things they do differently.

They do not dwell on negative emotions, but instead, they make efforts to rid their minds of them. Strong emotions will cloud your sense of intuition, mostly negative emotions. When you are upset, your thinking is blurred, and you are not yourself. People who have instincts do have real emotions and get angry; they choose not to hold onto the feeling.

They find the time to unplug from the world and spend time relaxing. Burnout, stress, and always being busy will stifle your intuition. You will still feel an impulse about the people around you, but if you do not take the time periodically to relax, your mind will be too tired to recognize your intuition for what it is.

Dreams are something to be remembered and analyzed. By paying attention to your dreams, you will become more in touch with your unconscious mind's thinking processes. This process will help you reach into the part of your mind that feeds your intuition. During the night, the intuitive or unconscious part of your brain provides information to other parts of your brain. You will gain a lot of information on how to live your life by paying attention to your dreams.

While reading other people's minds might seem like something from fantasy, it is something that most people do every day. Watch the body language, emotions, and words of another person, and you will be displaying empathetic accuracy. This feeling resembles what happens when you are watching an image of a spider crawling, and you feel a crawly sense on your skin or the way you feel sadness when you watch someone else being rejected. Lust, disgust, embarrassment, pride, and shame are all social emotions you can feel by watching someone else experience them.

Intuitions can cause physical sensations in the body, and people who use intuition regularly know to pay attention to these symptoms. People with intuition are naturally nosy people who pay attention to everything that is going on around them. They notice when strange things happen, even if they are only small events. If you pay attention to circumstances around you, you will begin to grow the connections that will help you develop your intuition.

Another excellent way to tap into the powers of your mind is to practice being more mindful, and meditation is one of the best ways in which to do this. When you are aware, you can tune into your intuition, objectively weigh your options, filter out chatter from your mind, and then come to a reasonable conclusion that you will feel comfortable honoring. You can also boost your self-knowledge by practicing mindfulness, and this will also help you connect to your intuition better. Meditation will help you with peace, creativity, compassion, and intuition.

The best creativity is done intuitively. Most sincerely, creative people are highly intuitive. They seem to know what is needed for any particular situation. If you improve your powers of creativity, you will automatically improve your powers of intuition. If you do not take time out for quiet, you will not be able to use your intuition. Spending time in solitude will help you connect to your inner wisdom, and it can also help you think more creatively. You need time to engage in deep thought and connect with yourself again. Your intuition will not work correctly if you are always surrounded by craziness.

Possibly the most essential trait that intuitive people have is that they listen to that little voice inside their heads. Gut feelings and intuitions are used to guide them. Some people refuse to pay any attention to their intuition even though everyone is connected to their intuition. Not everyone wants to admit that they listen to voices inside their heads freely. But you need to use a balance of rational thinking and intuition to make the best decisions. Intuition bridges the gap between reasoning and instinct. Do not listen to any cultural biases that speak against following your own best ideas from your intuition; if you genuinely seek this balance, you will be able to use all of your brain's resources to make your intuition better.

Psychic Ability

Psychomancy is the derivative of two Greek words, mancy, which means to detect secret things or to know things, and psycho, which is the word for mind, soul, and understanding. So the name Psychomancy translates to psychic sense or receiving impressions with the Astral Senses. Besides having five physical senses of touch, taste, smell, hearing, and seeing, you also have five astral senses. These astral senses only operate on the Astral Plane, which is the plane just above man's physical plane. You can use your Astral Senses to sense objects outside of you without using your physical senses. By using these Astral Senses, you are practicing Psychomancy.

The Astral Senses of Smell and Taste do exist, although they are rarely used. If you use your Astral Sense of Seeing, you will be able to do many things related to an elevated sense of sight. You will be able to see scenes and events that are distant to you, and some that may be very far away. You might be able to see through solid objects or see other things, like records of things that happened in the past or coming events from the future. All events that are coming your way will cast their shadows on the present time, so you may be able to know of them before they arrive. When you use your Astral Sense of Hearing, you will be able to tune into cosmic vibrations from far away or some from the past, since the waves will live on for many years after the original sound.

Astral Feeling is perhaps the most used of the astral senses. With it, you have the power to become aware of certain events on the Astral Plane. You might also be able to receive impressions from a far distance, both mental and emotional feelings. The Astral Sense of Feeling is more of an awareness of emotion than feeling the same passion emanating from the event. The Feeling can also be referred to as Sensing, as it is not the same as touching on the physical plane. There are still many instances of active feeling on the Astral Plane. Psychomancy can often feel the other entity's actual pain, known as taking on the condition or having sympathetic problems.

To truly understand the Astral Senses, you need to understand the idea of the Astral Body. Everyone has an Astral Body, and it is the counterpart of their perfect physical body. The Astral Body is held inside of the person's physical body and can only be removed with incredible difficulty. There are occasions when the Astral Body will leave the physical body, such as when you are dreaming or in times of overt mental stress. At these times, your Astral Body will leave you, and it will travel on extended journeys. It will move through space faster than the speed of light. The Astral Body remains connected to your physical body by a filmy connecting link. While it is difficult to separate the Astral Body from the physical body, an occurrence which usually involves the death of the physical body, the Astral Body is free to roam as it pleases as long as the filmy connecting link stays in place. This link is quite challenging to break, so the Astral Body can safely travel the Universe. It will visit different events and sense the feelings of those involved in the event.

Psychomancy as a practice lies dormant in everyone, and only those who choose to develop the ability will fully use it. All people possess the Astral Senses, but not all people know how to use them. The degree of development of your powers will determine the degree of the strength of your abilities. Premonitions and intuition are levels of Astral Sense. If your thoughts are too mired to pursue worldly life, it will be more difficult for you to awaken your Astral Senses. But there are methods you can adopt that will help you to awaken your Astral Senses and develop your Psychomantic Power.

You must first learn to concentrate and hold your attention fixed on one object for an extended time. When you are beginning, the easiest way to test your powers is to focus on an item that is familiar to you, like a book or a pencil. Hold the object in your hands, study its details, examine every part of the object until you have seen and noted every part of it. Now put the item aside and go on about your day. In two or three hours, come back to the object and repeat the exercise, and you will be surprised to learn that there are things you will notice the second time you did not see the first time.

When you have become adept at concentration, you can learn to visualize. This practice involves forming mental pictures of people, places, or things far away from you. It would help if you practiced this until you can bring up these scenes in your mind anytime you want. Another way to visualize is to sit as though you were planning to meditate and then mentally go somewhere you have been before. See yourself traveling the same route that you traveled initially and going to the same places again, all in your mind. Then you will use visualization to try to visit those places that you have never actually seen in person.

Once you have developed your concentration and visualization, then you will work on Psychometry. This exercise will involve taking an object that belongs to another person, something personal to them that they have worn like a hair ribbon or a ring. You will need to relax in a passive and receptive mental state, rest the item against your forehead, and close your eyes. Now let your Psychomancy tell you the history of the object, where it has been, and the events it has seen. Take your time because this is not a process that can be rushed. Wait calmly, and you will begin to receive impressions about the person who owns the object as you start to form a mental picture of them. This practice will take patience and perseverance because it is a new skill that you are learning, and it will not be hurried or rushed.

Divinity and the Divine

The state of being connected directly to the source is the state of divinity. When your heart is full of caring, compassion, and love for your fellow-creatures in the Universe, then you are said to be in a state of divinity. This state allows your mind to fill with happiness, peacefulness, joy, and patience. When you are completely relaxed and feeling compassion, creativity, joy, focus, and energy, you are in a divinity state.

Divinity might mean something entirely different from one person to another. You spend a large part of everyday analyzing what you learn from your five senses. You see, hear, smell, taste, and touch the world that spins around you. You create an internal focus of all of your awareness. Sometimes you might think that the reality that you see outside of you is all that exists because what happens outside will command all of your attention if you let it. If you take the time to become a passive observer of the external reality and spend more time on the inner impressions you have gathered, you will be closer to your divinity. When you work with these impressions, they will guide you on the path to your role in creation. Along with your Spirit, you will find your place in the Universe where you will begin to create the essence of your own Inner Being. You will use the inner thoughts that you feel are the most appropriate for your journey. Then you can make an external reality in the style that you prefer.

There is divinity in all people, not just in those who personally walk with their choice of a higher being. The divinity inside of a person is the more significant part of who a person is. Your physical body is the smaller outside expression of the larger inside reality of the person you are. The important thing is to find your method for creating a relationship with your inner divinity, your real source of being. At any time, you can change and update the impressions that make your inner divinity.

Meditation works for awakening the divinity that waits inside of you. When you meditate, all of the waves of your brain are synchronized to work together. Meditation will enhance the integration of your mind with your body. When your divinity is awakened through meditation, then you will immediately gain more insight and clarity. Making decisions alone and knowing what things will harm and what things are right for you will be more comfortable. You will stop wasting energy through needless arguments because you will be better able to express how you feel. Divinity will help you show respect for others, and this is the key to any good relationship because care translates into trust.

All people have inherent gifts that they are born with. If you develop your divinity with meditation, you will be better able to tap into these gifts and use them. You will expand your interests and offerings and find your inner source of these gifts. You will also be able to create valuable positive change in the world around you. Creativity and innovation are deeply interrelated with divinity. When you innovate, you will bend some rules in your quest for free exploration. You will be able to diversify your world and have a little fun without always looking for the immediate answer. Divinity will give you the power to connect with seemingly unrelated information to form your reality. When divinity is awakened, it will help you build your creativity and innovation. You will also learn that you are more thoughtful and insightful when you have revived your divinity. You will be able to succeed in your efforts because you will now understand all situations from the vantage point of a higher perspective. The change will not happen overnight, but it will be worth all of the work you put into it.

Knowledge of Angels and Spirits

You might have heard of angels, archangels, guardian angels, and spirit guides, and these terms are often used interchangeably, which is not correct. An angel and a spirit guide are not the same, and angels come in many different levels.

Everyone has a spirit guide that is always there to help you on your journey through life. Your spirit guide is a soul that has left its human body and has reached a certain point in their evolution. They are then expanded enough and aware enough to have the ability to lead you through your journey of life. Your spirit guide has been incarnated on earth as a human being, so they can completely understand your human experience. They will give you the love, compassion, and a certain level of non-judgment that most people will only be able to dream about.

Anyone who is a spirit guide has agreed to assume the role of being a spirit guide. Not only is it their job to assist you, but they also want to assist you. The secret to the spirit guide is that they need you to ask them for help because they cannot assist you if you do not. When you ask your spirit guide for guidance, their support is assistance, but if you have not requested yet, then their intervention would be viewed as interference, which is not allowed. You will want to find a way to create a relationship with your spirit guide and learn how to connect with them.

Your spirit guide will fulfill different roles in your life. And you have more than one spirit guide since you will require different types of assistance at other times in your life. And in times of trauma, you can ask for, and receive, the help of a spirit guide who is particularly adept at the kind and level of assistance that you need at that moment. And while spirit guides are always human, you might also have a spirit animal that will act as a protector or a companion or even a conductor of wisdom.

An angel is different from a spirit guide, and various spiritual traditions will describe the angelic's realms in different ways. All of the practices seem to agree that angels come in hierarchies and are organized into groups by their function. Angels are available for protection and guidance, just like your spirit guide is, and they will also provide you with wisdom, compassion, and unconditional love. Unlike spirit guides, it is not believed that angels have ever been incarnated in any form other than the angel.

You will not worship an angel, but you are allowed to pray to them and talk to them. Some believe that everyone has one guardian angel whose job it is to watch over them all during their lives. Your guardian angel will keep you safe in dangerous situations, and they will use your powers of intuition to steer you away from choices that might be dangerous. A guardian angel is a type of spirit guide in angel form. Your guardian angel is presumed to be the direct expression of the love that God has for you individually. The assumption is that God sent the guardian angel to watch over you during your life. They are full of pure love, and they will encourage you, protect you, guide you, and help you achieve the best possible qualities lying dormant in your soul. They come to you just before you are conceived, and they will remain with you until you pass on to the other life. They are right beside you for every thought, word, and event of your life. They are committed to completing your entire journey with you, and you are the only human they will have while you are alive.

You should try to make conversation with your guardian angel even if you have never seen any concrete proof of their existence. Have patience while you are practicing your communication with them. Practice imagining, envisioning, sensing your guardian angel, listening to them, and intending to see them in your dreams. You will be able to detect their presence even more clearly. Eventually, you will be able to sense their presence, hear them speak to you in your mind, and you may also come to know their name. You can become to know your guardian angel by asking them for some form of assistance. Always treat your guardian angel in the same manner as you would treat your dearest friends.

The most well-known of all of the angels are the archangels. While there are probably hundreds of angels, there are many fewer archangels. They will all have their specific area of expertise, such as the archangel of healing or protection. Depending on your religious affiliation, you may believe in the presence of three, seven, fifteen, or even another particular number of archangels. Angels who have proven their worth will be exalted to the rank of an archangel. You will have an archangel assigned to you, just as you will have an angel assigned to you, but since there are fewer archangels than angels, you will not have your archangel. The job of the archangels is to manage the lives of humans here on earth. This will include keeping order in the natural world, helping souls develop spiritually, showing people how to walk on their path in life, creating and facilitating contracts for the soul, and many other functions. Every archangel will have their private specific area of expertise to help ensure all humans' best possible experience.

Archangels are appointed specially by God. Their job is to help humans as they journey through their lives here on earth. Archangels can be in more than one place at one time, and they will have a specific area of concentration. By asking for help from your archangel, you are acknowledging their presence. Also, by asking for their assistance, they will be able to attribute their support to the love of God.

It is not needed to have a special prayer when you are asking for help from your archangel. You can even just initiate a conversation with your archangel to start contact. Your archangel will appear to you differently from how they will appear to other people. Your own experiences with your archangel will be uniquely personal and will be dependent on your own experiences.

Seeing the Aura of Others

The human body has many fields of energy. These include the body as a whole and the magnetic and electromagnetic fields generated by all living organs, tissues, and cells. There are also biofields, which are subtle fields that emanate from the human body. The morphogenetic areas are concerned with the energy that emanates purely from the physical body. There are also the etheric fields and the particular energy fields.

Etheric is the word that is often used to describe the aura of a person or their subtle body. Every vibrating unit of life has its independent etheric field, including persons, plants, and even the tiniest cell. There is also a specific field connected to the body as a whole, which is known as the particular energy field. The word etheric is derived from the word ether, a medium that can transmit waves of energy as it permeates space. When it is associated with the full auric field, it will surround the entire body, which is why it is part of the human's energy field.

The etheric body links the subtle body with the physical body. This energy field for the human body exists before the cells begin to grow, and it also permeates every particle of the human body.

The specialized energy fields refer to the areas that surround the biofields of the body. These biofields regulate the various physical, spiritual, emotional, and mental functions in the human body. The physical field is the lowest in frequency, and it governs the operations of the human body. The etheric field is the blueprint for the structure of the body that it is surrounding. The dynamic field regulates the emotional state of the person. Beliefs, thoughts, and ideas are processed in the mental area. The next site is the astral field, and it is free of space and time as it acts as the link between the spiritual and the physical realms. Existing only on the spiritual plane and holding the highest ideals for existence is the etheric template. The celestial field serves as a template for the etheric fields and accesses the energies of the Universe. And the lower levels of existence are regulated by the causal field.

People have long been substantiating through investigation the existence of the human aura. The aura is the energy field that surrounds all human beings, with everyone having their unique atmosphere. This field is created from many energy bands that are known as the auric fields or the auric layers. These layers connect you to the world outside of your body and encompass the entire subtle body. Other cultures refer to the aura by different names. Some refer to it as a cosmic light, and some depict it as a glow that encircles their religious icons in a circle of light.

The Eastern religions' spiritualists have much information on the aura and have written about it for centuries.

If you can see the energy field that surrounds another person, then you see their aura. The existence of the aura is real, but the way it is interpreted will vary in different philosophies and practices. The aura around you is the electromagnetic field caused by the fact that you radiate a low level of electricity from the functions in your body. It is easy for some people to read the aura of another person, and for some people, it takes years of practice.

The tricky part of seeing an aura around someone else is reading it and gaining knowledge from what is read. The challenge is to decide what the truth is and what is not. You will use your emotional antenna to read the auras of other people. Considering what the colors mean is one of the essential considerations you will need to make, as the colors can invoke certain emotions. For some people, the color red might mean envy, malice, or hatred, and for other people, they may emanate this color if they are feeling passion or love. Follow your instincts when you are seeing the energy of another person. When you see the glow of power from another person, always think about what those colors might mean for you. You will need to decide if the aura you are seeing gives you the information you can share with others. Maybe the aura is offering solutions to a way that you can help that person strengthen, restore, or heal their aura. If there is nothing positive that you discern from reading the person's aura, then it might be better to keep your findings private. An aura can be weakened by disease, physical illnesses, loud noises repeatedly heard, stress and fear, negative emotions, and substance abuse or addictions.

Reading an aura can give you clues to the people around you. You are better able to react accordingly if you know the mood of a person. When you interact with other people, you will produce the desired outcome and create a more emotionally beneficial situation for you. An aura will never lie even if the person does. Think of the atmosphere as the fingerprint of the spirit. Auras will not be pretended because they reveal actual emotional and spiritual intent. The auras of some people are weakened, and their colors are not vibrant. When the person is filled with jealousy, hatred, envy, or anger, their auric field will be pale and weak. The effects of physical symptoms will appear in the aura long before they appear as an illness or disease in the body. You can also use your knowledge of reading an atmosphere to understand your aura. Then you can use the knowledge that you find there to heal yourself when healing is needed.

Visiting Parallel Dimensions

The idea of a parallel dimension or universe is often thought of as the domain of science fiction movies. But scientists have been tossing around the idea of the existence of other dimensions for many years, and all for one simple reason. The level of quantum matter is the smallest level of value in reality, and for some reason, it is erratic and unstable. Since it is the matter, it should, theoretically, be stable. But scientists who studied the quantum level noticed that the particles in this tiny world have the capacity to change shape and move into other forms. This finding is why the possibility of other worlds' existence is not an unreasonable idea. If the quantum matter can achieve different states, it must exist on two other planes if it can exist as two separate states of matter. The universe will split when an action has more than one possible outcome, such as the quantum matter taking different shapes.

The theory proposes that if you have ever found yourself as taking part in an event where death is a possible outcome, you are dead in some other dimension. This concept of parallel worlds also disturbs the long-held belief that time is a linear thing. If this is true, then any timeline of events will be several timelines of the same event with all of the different possible outcomes. It is not possible to know if this theory is correct because there is no way that you can know yourself in this realm and another realm at the same time.

The parallel universe is one of the theories that make the idea of a multiverse more plausible. There exists some evidence that points to the possibility of a multiverse. Some trigger billions of years ago, whose origin remains unknown, caused the matter in space to inflate and expand. As the initial expansion began to cool down, the Big Bang's immense energy lessened, and light began shining through the small, floating particles. They began to gather and make pieces of matter that were progressively larger until planets, stars, and galaxies were formed. This leads to the question of how many universes exist in the cosmos. If the Big Bang could create the world you live in, it could easily make other universes. There are at least five theories that point to the complete probability that the multiverse exists.

The Infinite Universe – There is no way to know for sure the shape of time and space. It might be flat and infinite, so that gives rise to the possibility of many universes existing out there. But it is also possible that the same universe might exist more than once because particles can only arrange themselves in so many different configurations.

The Bubble Universe – This theory is based on the idea of eternal inflation. If you view space and time as a whole, you will see that some space areas will no longer inflate themselves while others will continue to grow larger. So if you envision the universe as being in a massive bubble, then there exists a network in the space of other worlds in drops. They might all have different physics laws than your universe does because the different bubbles are not linked.

The Daughter Universe – By following the laws of probability, you would see that every possible outcome of any decision you make would exist in its universe. That would create a wide range of galaxies that would all be one outcome of your decision. If you are trying to decide what to do with your life next year, you might develop many possibilities. You could get a job, go to school, get married, move to another country, or on the beach. In the Daughter Universes world, there would be one universe for every one of those possibilities, and you would be present in each one living a different life.

The Mathematical Universe – Another idea is that the universe's structure might depend on the design of the mathematics used to create it. A mathematical equation could be written to construct many different universes. Some would be populated, and some might not be.

The Parallel Universe – If space and time are flat, then there are a finite number of possibilities for the arrangement of particles to make a universe, but these arrangements are numerous. This arrangement would mean that each universe that is exactly like the one that you live in would be repeated many times over, with you in each one.

Déjà vu may be proof that other universes exist. The term déjà vu translates literally into already seen. This sense means you have a strong feeling that you have seen it before. If you have existed in another realm and noticed something, then your memory brought that thought out when you see it again, other parallel worlds may exist. After all, space and time are not precisely equal all of the time, so it is possible that you might be in one universe a split second before you are in another universe.

Life After Life

The life that comes after death, also known as the afterlife, is the belief that the human stream of consciousness or the essential part of the individual continues to live after the physical body's death. This vital part of the individual that remains to live on after death can either be the complete spirit or soul of the person or partially. It might carry the personal identity of the individual it came from. The continued existence is often believed to happen in a realm of the spiritual. It is thought that the individual's spirit will begin the cycle of life all over again by being reborn into the world. Those who are reborn will most likely have no memory of the life or lives they lived before. In rebirth theory, the deaths and rebirths might repeatedly happen until the individual is allowed to enter some otherworld or spiritual realm and stop returning in regeneration. Metaphysics, esotericism, and religion often drive significant views of the afterlife.

Most major religions profess some sort of belief in a continued existence after the physical body dies. This existence might be a continuation of the presence of the soul in a new life form. It might also be an eternity spent in a place of hellish punishment or a paradise full of peace and love. Any of these scenarios is part of the afterlife, and those who return from any of these places are the beings that come from the afterlife. Most religions not only have details on how your present life on earth will affect your life in the afterlife, but they profess detailed descriptions of what is to be expected in the afterlife. The majority of religions will teach about either Heaven and Hell or a belief in reincarnation.

Hinduism and Buddhism teach that all people will live more than one life and that most people will live many lives. The deceased's soul will reincarnate into another life after the death of the physical body. That next life will depend much on how that person conducted themselves in the previous experience. Karma determines where you will go in your next life according to the beliefs of Hinduism. Since the reincarnations are not clearly defined, it is understood that a person can return as almost anything. The opinions in Buddhism are more clearly defined. They believe that there are six possible realms that someone can go after death, and none of these realms are permanent. The domains consist of Asura, a state of constant arguing and fighting; hungry ghosts, which is the realm of continuous dissatisfaction; reincarnation as an animal; reincarnation as another human, the suffering of hell, or the paradise of heaven. These traditions teach that the constant cycle of life and death will never end until the soul reaches a point of peace and self-actualization.

Those who have been victims of unexplained events such as being tripped, hit, bitten, or pinched may have been the victim of a poltergeist. This phenomenon is usually explained as a troublesome spirit targeting a specific person and not a particular location, as a ghost who roams in a building does. They are also known to make knocking noises and move objects from one place to another. Almost every culture in the world has reports of the presence of poltergeists. These are malicious spirits who have no good intentions toward the target of their mischief. Followers of Spiritism believe that the manifestations of lower-level disembodied spirits are what become poltergeists. These lower-level spirits are closely associated with the world's natural elements, such as air, fire, earth, and water.

Spiritualism is a religious movement based on Spiritism and the belief that the dead do coexist with the living. In their ideas, the dead are inclined and able to communicate with the living. Spiritualists see the spirit world, the afterlife, as a place where spirits continue to evolve and not a static place devoid of change. Their belief that souls are more advanced than humans and continue to grow after death leads to the third belief that spirits can teach the living about God's nature and provide knowledge about ethical and moral issues. They believe that spirit guides are the specific spirits that are called upon for expertise and support.

Spiritualists believe that it is entirely possible to communicate with the discarnate humans, the deceased's spirits. They feel that anyone who wishes to put forth the effort can become a medium for the soul, and that spirit mediums are the ones who will communicate with the spirits. Spirits can attain perfection through growth, and they will progress through higher planes as they evolve. The spirits are ready to speak to anyone who will listen, but they will only formally communicate with a spirit medium.

Followers of Spiritism, on which Spiritualism is loosely based, take the belief in the spirits one step further. They believe that any living being is nothing more than an immortal soul inhabiting a physical form. They will continue through as many incarnations as they need to achieve intellectual and moral improvement. Spirits that have been disembodied may participate in the evil or beneficial influence of the physical world through either active or passive mediums. One of the main differences between the beliefs of the Spiritists and those who follow Spiritualism is that the Spiritists firmly believe in reincarnation.

The Spiritists' philosophy can be summed up by saying that people should do wrong to no one and try to do good to all peoples. The soul is born with its personality, and it will keep that personality through all of its incarnations. When the soul leaves the physical body after death, it will travel to the spirit realm where it will encounter all of the spirits it has faced before, and it will remember all of them. Spirits can influence both matters and think, and they use this influence to either harm or be useful in the physical world, depending on their soul's inherent personality.

The early cultures had methods of their own to cope with the idea of death by creating beliefs about an afterlife. They all believed that death is an inevitable part of life, thinking about an afterlife will help ease the pain of death, after death, the judgments for evil and suitable are made. There are multiple levels of punishment and reward in the afterlife. Death is not the end of life. A review of the other person's thoughts and their actions in life will determine what their afterlife will be.

Communicating With Others

Small particles of quantum matter from many other worlds seep into our world's fabric to interact with small particles of the quantum matter here. This seepage includes the particles that can communicate with other particles over great distances and those that appear to be in more than one place simultaneously. In any given world, these particles occupy a specific area. These places will vary between worlds, giving the particles of quantum matter the appearance of occupying several regions at once. And the quantum communication of particles from a faraway place is the result of the interaction between nearby worlds.

Most people believe that if someone is contacted by life from another world, then some extraterrestrial has landed in an unidentified flying object and contacted them. While this can happen and has happened, it is not how most of the contact is made. Human beings do exist in other worlds, other dimensions, at the same time, and they are capable of traveling consciously into and across dimensions. Many different cultures regularly use the out-of-body experience and astral projection for their own needs and their benefits.

Extraterrestrial beings are also multi-dimensional entities. If someone can travel to other dimensions, they will be able to make contact with the beings in these different dimensions. It seems that nothing is happening to their physical state. While anyone can learn to have an astral projection or other out-of-body experience, some people have developed a higher level in their consciousness. They can travel to even higher dimensions. This consciousness gives them the ability to gain access to the more advanced contact and knowledge available in other dimensions while also allowing them to perceive more of the different dimension's realities.

Entities from other dimensions have been roaming the earth for ages. They come in their flying craft that can only be seen by humans during times of astral projection. They are not here to harm humans; instead, they come in peace and are here to help the earth's people if they are allowed to. Like a wondrously great cosmic family that is highly advanced, they can communicate with humans, see humans without humans seeing them, and know the thoughts of the humans they are around. People naturally conclude that extraterrestrials do not exist because their minds are not open enough to receive contact from them. They will only approach those who will listen and are in a position or desire to help others.

Since all beings are multi-dimensional, it is an easy matter to communicate with beings in another world. When you have enjoyed a spiritual transformation and opened your Third Eye, you will become aware of various beings' presence. There are multiple beings everywhere, from the tiny beings in quantum particles to extraterrestrials to spirits to angels. When you awaken your spiritual senses, you will communicate with all beings, no matter their location. You might hear words sometimes, although most of the communication will be telepathic. Information is lost in the translation from one mind to another, but the largest part of the information will be shared. Inter-dimensional communication and telepathy are based more on feelings than words. You will need to be completely in touch with yours and accept your abilities if you want to have the ability to communicate with other dimensions.

CONCLUSION

Thank you for making it through to the end of *Kundalini Energy*; let's hope it was informative and able to provide you with all of the tools you need to achieve your goals, whatever they may be. You are prepared to walk a unique path in your life, and the energy that is residing dormant inside you will be the key to awakening all of your goals and dreams. This book guides you on the path to achieve that realization.

Your next step is to begin exploring your own powers and preparing to awaken your Kundalini. This energy has been present inside you since before you were born, and it will remain inside you until the day you die. In between those two momentous events, you should enjoy the power and fulfillment using this energy will bring to you. The power of the Universe is within your reach; you will need to reach out and take it. If you have never truly tested yourself, you have no idea of the amazing things you will achieve with the power of the Kundalini energy flowing through your body. You will become more grounded, happier, peaceful, and empathetic while learning the boundless limits of your new spirituality.

As the Kundalini begins to awaken inside you and you feel the energy of ancient wisdom coursing through your body, you will know a power that many people desire and few people ever truly experience. Awakening the Kundalini will require some work on your part. You must be willing to let go of the life you now know. You must be ready to reach out for something larger than yourself, something that people before you have understood and used to their advantage. You must be prepared to experience some discomfort, and maybe even pain and confusion, as you rid your mind and spirit of all of the stale ideas and old experiences that are currently holding you back.

Whenever you have an experience, good or bad, that experience leaves a mark on your spirit. It is almost like growing a callous over your heart. Every time that area is rubbed, the callous gets a bit thicker, until one day, it is impossible for any feeling to get through because the callous is so dense and impenetrable. When you begin the Kundalini awakening, you will be forced to strip away all of those old calluses that have built up over time. Layer by layer, all of the relics of your old life will be ripped off and left behind. This process can be painful, and it is the very reason why many people will not begin the journey, or they will stop in the cycle, simply because it is too painful. But the pain of removing all the old memories will eventually lead you to the life you want to know. You will not achieve anything real or right in your life until your heart and soul are free to feel the way they were always meant to feel.

Kundalini energy is the life force that will bring you to your true self-realization through transformation and spirituality. Once you have navigated the transformation, you will feel a freedom of spirit you have never before known. Your creativity and abilities will be unlimited, as there will no longer be any bond holding you back. Your soul will be lifted to soar to new heights previously only imagined by your mind. You are ready to make this journey. Everything you will need to complete your Kundalini awakening and begin to enjoy this energy is in this book, so go ahead and get started on your incredible new life path.

There will be nothing to stop you once you begin your transformation. The level of intuition and spirituality you might have only dreamed of previously will now be a reality. All of the realms of the Universe will be open to you, along with all of the power of the life force from the Kundalini.

Finally, if you found this book useful in any way, a review on Amazon is always appreciated!

DESCRIPTION

There are times in everyone's life when they feel lost and alone. Life might not seem to offer much in the way of hope and happiness. The stressful world outside has begun to creep in and disturb their inner peace and calm. The high hopes they had for a fulfilling life seem to fade a little bit more every day. If any of these sounds like you, then you have come to the right place, or at least to the right book.

Because this book, *Kundalini Energy,* is the place that you need to be to get your life back on track. You need to know the Kundalini's energy flowing inside you, and this book is the guide you will use to achieve that marvelous happening in your life. The issues that plague you physically, emotionally, mentally, and spiritually will all be resolved when you learn how to utilize the Kundalini's energy to make changes in your life. All of the details you need to know about your Kundalini and the power that will flow through you after your awakening is right here inside this book. You will see how you can enjoy:

- Enhanced psychic abilities
- Increased creativity
- Increased empathy
- The purity of your mind and soul
- Release of your full potential

It might not be easy to believe that something already presents inside you can wield so much power over your life, but your Kundalini energy can and will do just that. It has been present inside you since before you were born, and it will be with you until you die. In between those events, the Kundalini energy will drive you to the life you always knew was possible. Once you have taken the steps needed to awaken the vast potential inside you, there will be no limit to what you will be able to achieve. You will feel renewed in your spirit, with a greater sense of peace and tranquility. You will know your proper place in the Universe, and you will have the skills you need to achieve that place. And you will feel a greater empathy toward your fellow man.

There are other benefits to awakening your Kundalini. The energy of the Kundalini will cycle through you and take you to the heights of self-realization. Once you have completed the transformation and come to the level of true self-realization, there will be powers available to you that will allow you to:

- Know other astral planes
- Understand life afterlife
- Connect with the Divine
- Know the powers of the Universe

Your spiritual transformation will enable you to accomplish your goals and dreams. You will no longer feel so lost and alone, as your strength will come from within you. You will learn to create your hope and happiness, and the stresses of the outside world will no longer exert any effect over your life. Your life will be meaningful and fulfilling. All of the information that you need to know and all of the secrets that will help you achieve this are here in this book. So go ahead and click that BUY button and begin your journey to the upper realms of true enlightenment.

www.ingramcontent.com/pod-product-compliance
Lightning Source LLC
Chambersburg PA
CBHW081348070526
44578CB00005B/770